Build Your Own WordPress Website

The Ultimate Guide for Small Business Owners

Acknowledgements

A special thank you to Maria Antonietta Perna for her excellent contributions to the book. She has provided excellent ideas, content and wisdom and has been a pleasure to work with from start to finish. Our thanks also extend to Lucia Koloziova for her efforts and involvement in helping to provide the finishing touches to what we hope is the number one book on the market, for helping you build an attractive and successful website.

Cover by Kane Georgiou.

kane@thewordpressgenie.com
www.thewordpressgenie.com

TABLE OF CONTENTS

CHAPTER 1

Introduction

1.1 Why Having a Great Website is Important for Your Business

Having a strong online presence has become a must for all serious businesses. No matter if yours is a traditional brick and mortar shop or an edgy tech start-up, as a business owner you need a sleek, professional-looking website which tells your potential clients **who** you are, **what** you do, and **how** to get in touch with you.

Here are three compelling reasons why having an effective website is important.

Books are judged by their cover, and so is your business

Put yourself in the shoes of a potential client who's interested in what you have to offer. Let's face it, the first thing you would do is to head over to your friend Google and find out more about the company. Make sure your website is top-notch: prospects will pass judgment on your business largely based on the experience they have when they land on your website.

Shopping habits have changed: customers visit you online before they set foot in your shop

Most of your potential customers will have entered your online premises before making a decision whether or not it's worth their while to pay you a visit in person. Your website needs to **rank well on search engines** so that they can find you quickly. It also needs to **spell out your offer** and make it very **easy for people to get in touch with you**.

No website means fewer business opportunities coming your way

It should be clear by now that if people can't find you online, you'll be missing out on potential customers finding out about your business and deciding to spend money on what you have to offer. However, make no mistake about it: a *bad* website is worse than no website at all because it will make your business look bad. If you have a website and it looks like it was built in the '90s, doesn't display well on a mobile device, is slow to load and hard to read, there's only one thing for you do do: take it down and build a new one.

1.2 What You'll Find in This Guide

The team at thewordpressgenie.com wrote this guide to help you set up a professional and functional website for your small business. As a business owner myself, I faced the same challenge of having to create a sleek online presence for my physiotherapy practice, but didn't know how to go about it without spending a fortune on web agency services.

In this guide I'm going to take you through the same journey I made, without the pitfalls and mistakes I encountered along the way, and show you how you can easily create a professional looking website for your small business using WordPress.

I will tell you all you need to know to get your new website up and running in no time. Here's a breakdown of what you'll learn:

- how to choose a domain name and hosting;
- how to install WordPress and configure it through its dashboard to meet your needs;
- how to create and manage your website's content;
- how to choose the right theme and customize it for your brand;
- how to update and secure your website;
- how to optimize your website for search engines;
- how to integrate a mailing list and social sharing capabilities into your website;
- how to set up a small but fully functional online shop on your website.

I'll take you through the process step by step and you'll be amazed to find out how much fun and rewarding it is to see your own creation come to life and be accessible to everyone on the Internet.

1.3 Who Is this Guide for?

Are you a solopreneur or small business owner looking to establish a strong web presence? If your answer is a resounding 'Yes', then this guide is for you.

Let's be clear, this book is not aimed at seasoned web developers, nor will it turn you into one. In fact, you won't need to be a professional coder to build a website for your small business. If you're familiar with using a home computer for common tasks like creating files, downloading software, browsing the Internet, and using a text editor like Google docs or Microsoft Word, you know all you need to follow along and enjoy the ride.

1.4 Why Is WordPress Great for Your Business Website?

Never before has the web been more democratic. The skills to set up a website used to be the preserve of a few Geeky individuals who could make sense of esoteric programming languages which didn't make any sense to the layperson. These days the web offers a wide range of free and premium tools like WordPress, Wix, Squarespace, and more, which enable anyone who puts their minds to it to create a nice looking website in a few hours or days. However, it's sometimes hard to wrap your head around all these platforms and it's not clear how to go about choosing one over the other. Making the right choice is important: once your website is set up, moving it to another platform is not always straightforward, and this kind of move could bring with it some painful falls from Google's search results.

I've chosen WordPress for my personal website and thewordpressgenie.com, and here are a few reasons why this is a great choice for your business website too.

1. WordPress makes it easy to update and maintain your website without relying on a professional developer to do the job. The software boasts full content management capabilities, therefore you don't have to know HTML to add fresh content to your website. Also, updating to a new version of WordPress is quickly done with a mouse click.
2. The software is free. Clearly, I wouldn't put this as the main consideration for choosing WordPress, but the fact that it is free, without being cheap, is a factor that works in its favour.
3. There's an awesome community supporting WordPress. If you get stuck at any time while you're building your website, the WordPress.org online forums are there to help. WordPress code base is not proprietary but open source, which means that a wide and ever growing community of developers from all over the globe keeps testing, improving and pushing updates to the software. Obviously you can also head over to thewordpressgenie.com to see if we can help you too.
4. WordPress offers blogging capabilities out of the box, which means that you can easily keep your website content fresh, interact with your readers, and build a loyal

following, all of which is great for search engines and your bottom line. WordPress is not limited to blogging, however. You can easily extend it with available themes and plugins. Themes control the appearance of your website to make it look anyway you want and plugins add more functionality, e.g., e-commerce, contact forms, sliders, etc. You'll learn about both later on in this guide.

5. Accessibility and Search Engine Optimization (SEO) are pretty much baked into the platform. Accessibility is about making your content accessible by everyone: people with vision and/or motor impairments, people visiting your website on small devices, as well as search engine crawlers. Surely, the more visitors can access your website the more value you'll be able to deliver, which means growth in business opportunities. SEO is about your website's visibility in search engine listings so your clients can easily find you. WordPress handles both very well and you can easily make it even better with the right plugins, which I will discuss later in the book.

Finally, the **freedom of being master of your own website** was the clincher that persuaded me to choose WordPress over all other user-friendly platforms for Do-It-Yourself website owners like me. On your WordPress-powered website you'll be free to grow your audience, sell your products, publish your content, etc., never fearing that the service is going to stop or change its terms: you decide your own terms.

It's time to know a bit more about this awesome platform.

1.5 What Is WordPress?

A visit to the WordPress.org website is the best place to find out what WordPress is all about. Here's a great definition:

> "**WordPress** is web software you can use to create a beautiful website, blog, or app. We like to say that WordPress is both free and priceless at the same time."

WordPress.org

WordPress started in 2003 and it's now grown to be the largest self-hosted blogging platform in the world. It's used to power millions of websites, from personal blogs to large-scale complex websites. I can safely say that WordPress is the most powerful open source blogging and content management system (CMS) software that is also easy to use and most suited to meeting your small business website's goals.

Difference between WordPress.org and WordPress.com

One distinction most beginners struggle to make is between WordPress.org and WordPress.com. Here's what you need to focus on.

The main difference lies in **who's hosting your website**. If you go for WordPress.org, *you* host your website. In other words, you purchase your domain name, buy a plan with a hosting company, download the WordPress software from WordPress.org and install it on your server. You'll find that most hosting companies offer a one-click install feature, installation instructions, and services to make the process as easy as possible for you.

With WordPress.com you are not responsible for web hosting or for downloading and installing WordPress or any of the plugins and themes. This is all taken care of for you. You can buy a domain name if you want, but it's not necessary. In fact, you can freely use the WordPress.com domain name together with your website's name, although this wouldn't look very professional on a business website.

There are pros and cons to both solutions, but in this guide I will show you how to set up an awesome WordPress.org website for your small business.

First things first: let's start by getting a domain name.

CHAPTER 2:

Setting Up Your WordPress Website

In this chapter I'm going to guide you through a number of core tasks involved in building a website. Here's what you're going to do:

- Choosing and register a domain name
- Purchasing a hosting plan
- Installing WordPress
- Doing some configuration and cleaning up tasks just like the pros.

Let's begin!

2.1 How to Pick and Register a Domain Name

Every website that is live on the Internet has a domain name. Without being too technical, a domain name is an easy way to reach the exact location of a website. For example, the domain name for the WordPress software website is: wordpress.org.

A domain name consists of a **top-level** and a **second-level** domain. A top-level domain (TLD), also known as *domain extension*, is the part of the domain name placed to the right of the dot ("."). In our WordPress example, the TLD is *.org*. The most common TLD is *.com*, and a very trendy one these days is *.io*.

The second-level domain (SLD) is the part of the domain you find to the left of the dot ("."). In our wordpress.org example, the SLD is *wordpress*.

Because a domain name is how people find your website and know about your company, it's worth giving your choice some careful thought.

Here are some tips on how to choose the best domain name.

Be unique, be specific, be relevant

The most important aspect of a domain name is its **availability**. If a domain name is taken, you can't use it. To minimize the chances of going wrong, being original is the way to go. Build uniqueness into your brand, and make your domain name reflect who you are and what your business is about.

Using a specific **keyword** can also help you with search engines ranking when people look for your type of business on line.

Being relevant is also important. Unless you're already a well-known brand, including a keyword making clear what your business is about will help people and search engines know what you do.

Let's say you're a guitar teacher who provides private tuition in the London area of Battersea. Now, let's come up with a few general ideas about a domain name and then narrow them down to something more unique and specific.

- musicteacher.com, musictuition.com or musictutor.com: not great, too general, most likely unavailable.
- londonmusicteacher.com, londonmusictuition.com or londonmusictutor.com: better, but still too general. London is a big city and music teacher is not specific enough
- learnguitarinbattersea.com or yourbatterseaguitartutor.com: these domain names convey some specific information about your business to people living in the London Borough of Battersea who want to learn how to play guitar. When they type something along the lines of 'Battersea guitar tutor' in a Google search, chances are your website will make it to the top of the search results or thereabouts.

On the other hand, if your brand is yourself, using **your name as your website domain name** is also a good option to consider. It's certainly unique, and when people look for you online, it's likely your website will turn up as number one on the search engines list.

Be memorable

As a small business, a hefty chunk of your business comes through word of mouth, so you should make it as easy as possible for your customers to recommend you to others. **It's more likely people talk about your business if your domain name is catchy and easy to remember.**

Try to avoid dashes and numbers

It's not that dashes and numbers in a domain name are inherently bad. For example, css-tricks.com is one of the most popular websites for front-end developers, despite the dash in the domain name. However, dashes and numbers often lead to typing errors or incorrect use, which could result in making your website harder to remember and even look less reputable.

What about Domain Extensions?

The best choice you can go for is a .com domain, simply because it's the most common. If you buy a .com domain, see if you can get your hands on the .net and .org versions as well and redirect them to your website on the .com extension.

If a .com is not available, the next best choice is a .net and .org.

There are tons of other possibilities like .pro, .me, .info, etc. I wouldn't make them your first choice because it's likely your customers aren't too familiar with them. What you're really after here is for people to easily remember and find you online and a quirky extension lends itself to typos and forgetfulness.

Buying Your Domain Name

It's common for website hosting companies to offer domain registration. This is the easiest option, because your hosting provider will take care of configuring your domain name to work with your website hosted on their servers. Besides, most well-known hosting companies offer free domain registration together with a hosting plan.

For more advanced users, or for those who are willing to invest in a professional webmaster, buying the domain name and hosting separately from different providers has a few advantages.

- In case you decide to switch your host, it'll be easy for you to do so without affecting your domain. Just move your files to the new host and configure your domain name to point to your website's new location.
- Not all hosting companies are great domain registrars and vice versa.
- Suppose you have multiple domains for different websites and you're using different web hosts for them. In this case, keeping all your domains in one place makes it easier for you to manage them.

Because I assume you're just starting out and this is your first website, I recommend you register your domain with your hosting provider. It will be up to your web host to configure your domain name to work with your website.

On the other hand, if you'd rather register your domain with a different company than your hosting provider, I recommend you choose a well-established registrar. GoDaddy.com is a great example of a suitable company for domain name registration. You'll find links to some useful tutorials on how to configure your domain to work with your website in the resources at the end of this guide.

2.2 Choosing WordPress Hosting for Your Website

Hosting is the physical computer where your website lives. It serves your files to your website visitors. In other words, you can't have a website without a host.

I can't stress enough how important hosting is to the success of your business website. Good hosting means a speedy website and minimum downtime, which will delight both your customers and search engine crawlers. However, going through all the hosting options can be confusing and working out the minimum requirements for a good WordPress hosting provider sounds kind of technical, which ends up putting a lot of people off.

Here I'm going to keep things simple and give you just what you need to know to make a great choice for your website.

These are three choices open to you:

- Shared hosting
- VPS hosting
- Managed WordPress hosting

I'll touch on each of them in turn.

Shared hosting

A great place to start as a small business is to hop on a shared hosting plan. This option enables you to get up and running in no time on a relatively **low budget**.

With a shared hosting plan, your website shares the server resources, e.g., memory, computational power, etc., with other websites.

The main advantage of several websites sharing the same server is that it keeps costs down for both you and the hosting company. The main disadvantage is that if some of the websites hosted on the same server consume more resources, this can result in slowing down other websites, including yours. Also, as your business website grows and traffic increases, you're likely to need more server resources. This won't be a big problem, though. It just means you'll need to upgrade to a different plan or a new hosting provider.

Among the kind of business websites making the most of affordable shared hosting are design agencies, small e-commerce sites, solopreneur websites like freelancers and small businesses, especially at the start of their activity.

If you think shared hosting meets your needs, you can choose from a number of available companies. Make sure you test their support services - with shared hosting, support is your number one asset.

VPS hosting

VPS stands for **Virtual Private Server.** The hardware is still shared like in shared hosting, but it's partitioned equally among a few users only. For instance, if the server hosts four accounts, each one may use only 25% of the resources. This means that decrease in speed or downtime issues due to some of the websites on the same server eating up more than their fair share of server resources are not likely to happen.

Besides being highly reliable, VPS hosting is also quite flexible. Let's say you'd like to try out other content management systems such as Joomla or Drupal, VPS gives you this kind of freedom.

VPS is certainly an option to consider for your business website if:

- you have the budget
- your business is mainly online
- you need to plan for future growth
- and if you or someone on your team knows their way around website maintenance and security.

Managed WordPress hosting

Managed hosting has the huge advantage of offering a totally **hassle-free** experience. In this scenario, the server is perfectly tuned to work with WordPress as efficiently as possible. Furthermore, such tasks as installing WordPress, website security, caching, updates and support are all benefits that come with this kind of hosting solution: it's the hosting provider, not you, who takes care of it all.

On the downside, you don't have much flexibility: you can't install other CMS platforms (but why would you want to?), for security and optimization reasons you can't freely install your own plugins and themes, in short you're quite limited to what the host allows you to do with your website.

As your business and your website grow and you don't know much about website maintenance and security, or you have better things to do than looking after the technical side of having a website, opting for this kind of solution could be great for small businesses: although it comes at a price, it's probably less than paying for a webmaster's services.

In this guide I assume you're just starting out and need to set up a website on as low a budget as possible. In this case, the best option is going for a reliable, well established and affordable shared hosting solution. While this means you're keeping costs low, it also means a hands-on approach on your part.

Once you're set up with a hosting account and a domain name, your next task is to install WordPress itself.

Let's dive in.

2.3 Installing WordPress

WordPress boasts a <u>famous five minute installation</u> feature. But you only need it if you decide to install the software manually. Most hosting providers offer one-click install tools that make installing WordPress a breeze.

Here, I'm going to cover the following two options:

- the **one-click install** tool on HostGator, a popular web hosting provider. Other well established hosts offer automatic installation tools that work in a similar way;
- **manually** installing WordPress on your server. This is a good chance for you to get acquainted with the file structure on your remote server where your website is hosted, which can be a useful skill to have.

Let's get started!

One-click install on HostGator

Once you're signed up with a hosting company, you'll have access to your control panel, which puts you pretty much in control of your own website.

Like most control panels in popular hosting companies, the HostGator control panel is very intuitive and easy to use. You'll find all related features grouped in their own specialized section, which makes finding your way around the panel a snap.

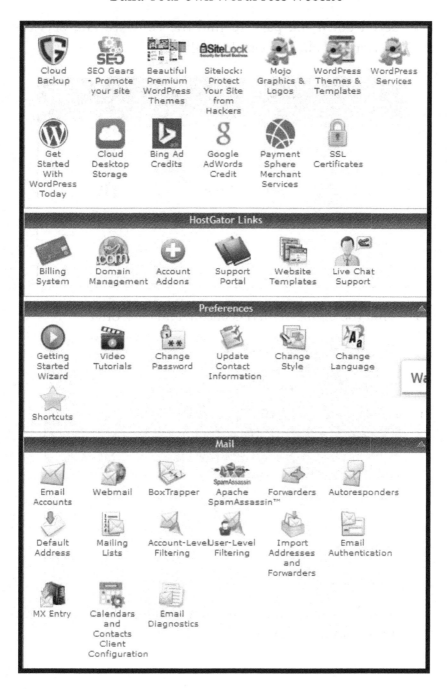

Once you're on your control panel, follow these simple steps.

1. Scroll down the page to find the Software and Services section and click on QuickInstall

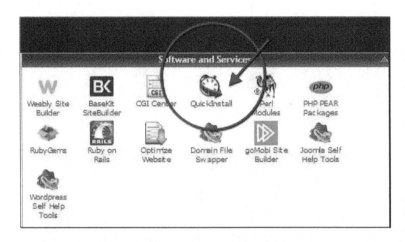

2. Find the *Install WordPress* button and click on it

You'll be presented with a few options. Simply pick the free installation option.

3. After clicking the *Install WordPress for FREE* option, you'll be presented with a simple form.

The first form field asks you for the file path on your server where you want your WordPress website to be

Build Your Own WordPress Website

installed. Don't be scared, just click the black down arrow and you'll find the path ready to be selected.

You'll also notice a '/' symbol after the path. If you want your website to go into a particular directory other than the root directory, then type that directory in the textbox following the '/' symbol. For instance, let's say you'd like your website URL to look like:

http://yourdomain.com/mywebsite

In this case, you'll type 'mywebsite' in the textbox after the '/' symbol.

However, I recommend you leave the textbox blank, which will result in the installation of WordPress in the root directory of your server. This means that when your visitors browse to http://yourdomain.com, they'll land on your website's homepage.

The other fields are pretty straightforward. Just fill out the form and click the *Install WordPress* button. The service will now run and install both WordPress and a database on your server.

4. Once the installation is complete, you'll get a confirmation message informing you that all has gone according to plan.

Now click the *View Credentials* button on the top right corner and you'll see the URL to your WordPress dashboard, your username and password. Just take note of your credentials and log into your website. Once inside, it should look something like this.

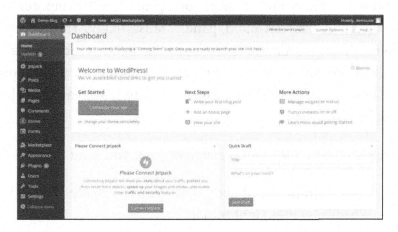

Congratulations, you now have a shiny WordPress website!

The Famous WordPress Five-minute Install

As nice as using an automatic installation software can be, not all hosting companies offer this service. Or perhaps, you'd like to have more control over the entire process. In any event, installing WordPress manually is quite painless.

You need an FTP (File Transfer Protocol) program to transfer WordPress files to your server. I use FileZilla, a free and user-friendly software, but you're free to use whatever you prefer.

An FTP program needs to know your host, username and password to establish a connection with your server. You can easily get this information from the control panel your hosting provider has made available to you. If you have any doubts, ask your web host support staff for help.

Once the connection is up and running, you'll see the files and folders on your server displayed in the right pane of your FTP program. Files and folders on your local computer are displayed in the left-hand pane. Most likely, the directory where your WordPress files need to be installed is called public_html (or something similar, depending on your chosen web hosting service. Once again, if in doubt, ask your host help desk for more info).

Here's a step by step walkthrough of what you need to do.

1. Click **public_html** so that you're ready to upload WordPress files right into it.

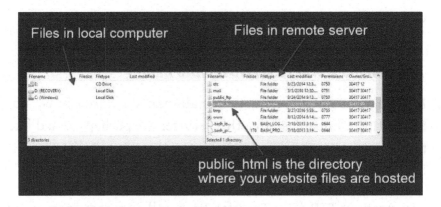

2. Go to the download page on WordPress.org and click the big Download WordPress button

This will download a compressed .zip folder containing all the WordPress files. Simply, unzip the folder in a location of your choice on your computer and browse to it from the left-hand pane of your FTP program. Make sure you click the directory called wordpress.

Doing so will give you access to all the files inside it from the FTP program.

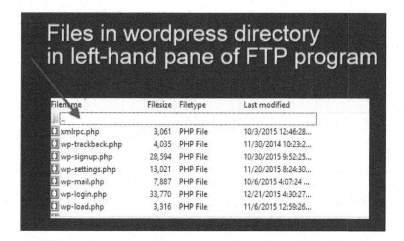

Make sure your FTP program is connected and its right-hand pane has public_html open. All you need to do now is to select all the WordPress files in the left-hand pane, then drag and drop them into the right-hand pane of your FTP program. Great! Now WordPress is on your server. Next, let's tackle the database.

3. WordPress handles your website content dynamically. This means that your content is stored in database tables and gets put together and served on the fly when your website loads into the browser. For this to work, you need to set up a database.

   From your hosting control panel, find the Databases section, then click on the *MySQL Databases* link.

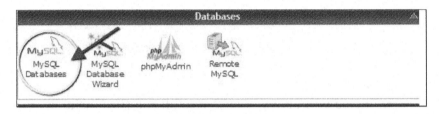

4. Now type a name for your database in the the textbox and click the *Create Database* button. Take note of your database name as WordPress will need it during the installation process.

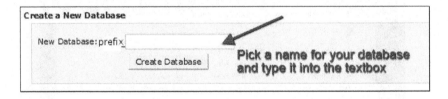

   For security reasons, the tool adds a prefix to everything you create on the database panel. The image above uses a dummy prefix, but if you're following along, you'll have your unique prefix.

5. Create a new database user by entering a username and password. Make sure you place both in a safe place as WordPress will need them during the installation process.

Click the *Create a User* button and proceed to the next section.

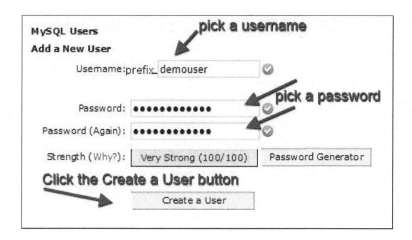

6. Add the new user to the database you've just created.

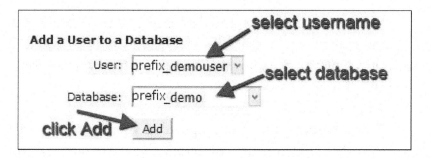

7. Next, add privileges to the database user by selecting the *All Privileges* checkbox and clicking the *Make Changes* button. Because this is the main user, grant all privileges. If you have more people managing your website, select your privileges carefully and only grant the minimum number necessary for that user to perform a given task.

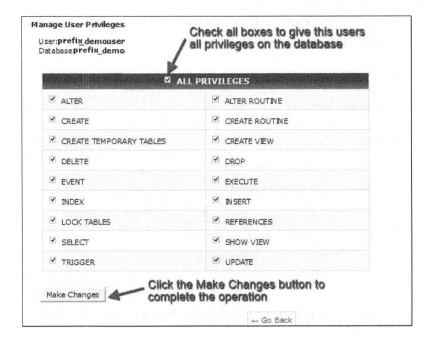

You're now done with the database. It's time to dive into installing WordPress itself.

8. Open your favorite browser and navigate to your website's URL, for instance:

http://yourdomain.com

If you followed along and uploaded your WordPress files into the public_html directory, you should see this language screen. Simply select your language from those available and click the *Continue* button.

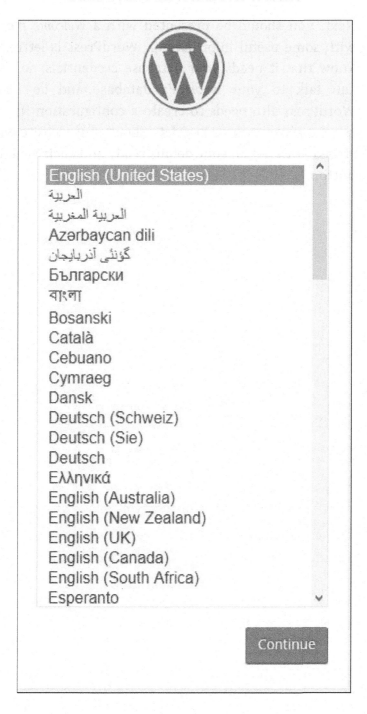

9. Next, you should be presented with a *Welcome* message with some useful information. WordPress is letting you know that it needs your database credentials, so that it can talk to your website's database and do its job. WordPress also needs to create a configuration file, wp-config.php, where key data about your website will be stored. Just get all your details ready and click the *Let's go* button.

Welcome to WordPress. Before getting started, we need some information on the database. You will need to know the following items before proceeding.

1. Database name
2. Database username
3. Database password
4. Database host
5. Table prefix (if you want to run more than one WordPress in a single database)

We're going to use this information to create a wp-config.php file. **If for any reason this automatic file creation doesn't work, don't worry. All this does is fill in the database information to a configuration file. You may also simply open wp-config-sample.php in a text editor, fill in your information, and save it as wp-config.php. Need more help? We got it.**

In all likelihood, these items were supplied to you by your Web Host. If you don't have this information, then you will need to contact them before you can continue. If you're all ready...

Let's go!

Now WordPress displays a form where you're going to enter your website's database details.

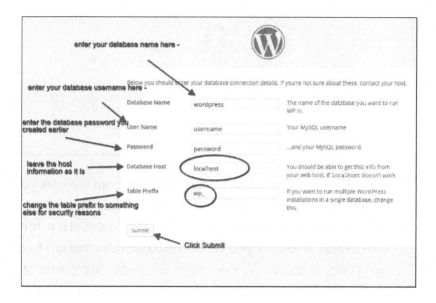

You should have the Database Name, database User Name and database Password that you created earlier in your control panel. Simply enter the details in the appropriate box.

Leave the *Database Host* box as it is, unless your hosting provider has given you a different name than localhost.

I recommend you **change the Table Prefix to something different from wp_** (e.g., dgxy_), even though you're only going to have just one WordPress installation. This is a security measure against hacking attacks. In fact, hackers know the default prefix for database tables in WordPress is wp_, and this information can help them find some unauthorized access to your database.

Finally, click the *Submit* button. WordPress should give you a reassuring message to let you know that it can now connect to your database and it's ready for the famous 5-minute install.

All right, sparky! You've made it through this part of the installation. WordPress can now communicate with your database. If you are ready, time now to...

Run the install ◀──────── click Run the install button

Click the *Run the install* button and keep an eye on your watch - let's see if it really takes you five minutes.

10. The next screen presents you with the installation form. WordPress is asking you for some basic information to set up your website. Take note of your username and password (these are **NOT the same as your database Username and Password**), as you'll need them to log into your WordPress dashboard at the end of the installation process.

Once you've filled out the form, click the *Install WordPress* button and keep your fingers crossed.

If all has gone well, you should see a success message.

Congratulations! You've installed WordPress on your server. How long did it take?

As a final step, click the *Log in* button at the bottom of the success message and use your WordPress credentials to access your website's WordPress dashboard.

Once you click the *Log in* button, the screen should display your WordPress administration panel, which has all you need to manage your new website.

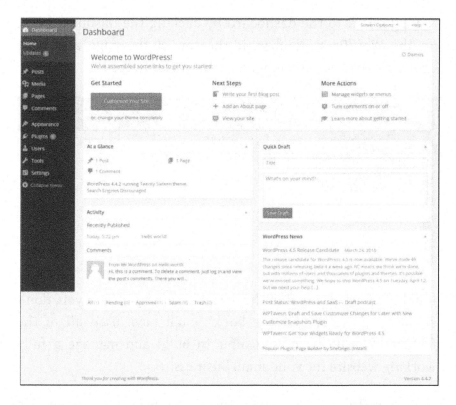

Now that your WordPress website is up and running, it's time for some very important post-setup tasks and checks. Most newbies make the mistake of skipping them. But not you.

2.4 Five Things You Need to Do after Installing WordPress

Now you're the proud owner of a brand new WordPress website. What a feeling! Take your time to visit your website on the front end: navigate to your website URL (e.g., http://yourdomain.com) and check that it looks fine. The latest default WordPress theme should be active and minimal default content should be displayed on the screen.

Next, go back to the dashboard by clicking the Dashboard link on the WordPress toolbar at the top of the page and start exploring the back end environment of your website.

If not all of what you find there makes much sense to you, don't sweat. By the end of the book, you'll have used all of the features WordPress has to offer to build and manage a fully working website for your small business.

New WordPress users simply stop at the installation stage, and think that picking a nice looking theme and adding some content concludes their website creation experience. Pros know better.

Here's a list of five important things you need to pay attention to immediately after installing WordPress.

#1 Make sure no user with the username Admin is present

You shouldn't have any user with the default name of *Admin*. That would be the very first username hackers will try when attempting to log into your WordPress website.

25

Instead, your username should be as cryptic as possible, so that hackers will have a hard time trying to guess what it is. If you think your Administrator username could be easily guessed and therefore should be changed, doing so is easy. Follow these steps.

● From your WordPress admin panel, click to Users -> All Users. The screen displays all the users and their roles on your website.

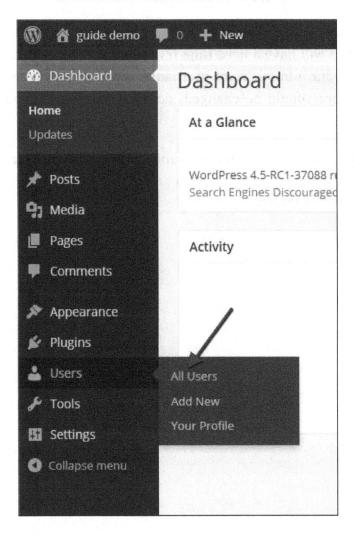

My Users screen looks like this.

At the moment, I have one user, called demouser, who's also the website's Administrator and hasn't authored any content yet. I created this user during the installation process. I'm logged into my website with this user's credentials.

Now that I know a bit more about WordPress security, I'd like to change this username into something the bad guys would find harder to guess. The next step is to create a new user and give this user the *Administrator* role (this is the role that gives absolute power over your website).

● Click on All Users -> Add New and fill in the form with the details for the new user. Make sure you **select Administrator from the Role drop-down box** and click *Add New User.*

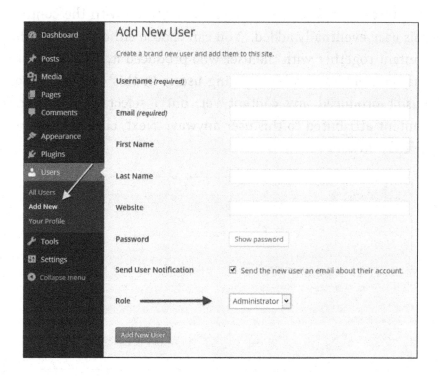

Now you have two Administrator users. Log out of the current Administrator account, which is the one you want to delete, and log in using the credentials of the new Administrator user, the one you just created. Simply select the previous Administrator user, in my case demouser, and click on the *Delete* link.

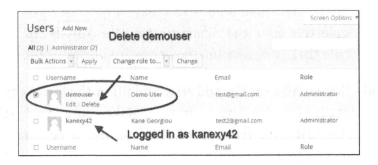

WordPress will ask you what you want to do with the content this user eventually added. You can choose either to delete the content together with the user who produced it, or to attribute that content to another existing user. In this case demouser hasn't produced any content yet, but I select to delete any content attributed to this user anyway. Next, click the *Confirm Deletion* button.

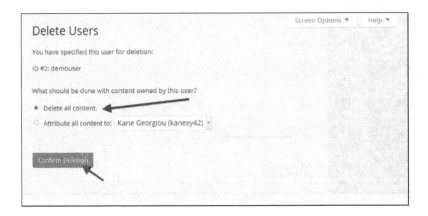

Great, you've just successfully changed the Administrator's username into something less hackable.

#2 Ensure your display name is different from your username

When you author a post or are logged in, WordPress displays your first and last name by default. If you want to change this, you can do so by going to Users -> Your Profile, select a different option from the drop-down box, and click the *Update Profile* button. However, don't use your username as your publicly display name. Doing so, makes it easier for hackers to attack your website.

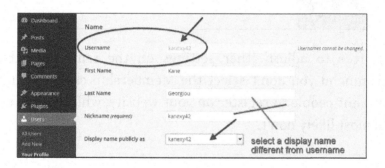

#3 Adjust WordPress Settings

There are at least three WordPress settings you need to configure at this point:

● Time zone
● Comments management
● Permalinks structure

Let's tackle each one in turn.

Setting the right time zone is important, especially if you want to publish posts automatically on a certain date and time. Go to Settings -> General and make the proper adjustments.

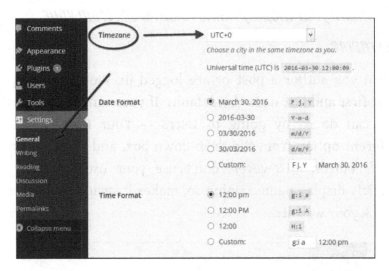

Feel free to adjust other settings on the same page, but I recommend you don't select the Membership checkbox unless you want people to register on your website, which at this stage you most likely don't.

When you're done, click the *Save Changes* button at the bottom of the page.

Next, you need to make sure you minimize the number of spammy comments on your website. As a preliminary measure, set WordPress to have comments manually approved before publishing them. Obviously, you'll need to keep an eye on the incoming comments on your website before they escalate to an unmanageable number. However, especially for new websites, this is not likely to be a concern.

You can easily adjust the appropriate setting by going to Settings -> Discussion and select the *'Comment must be manually approved'* option.

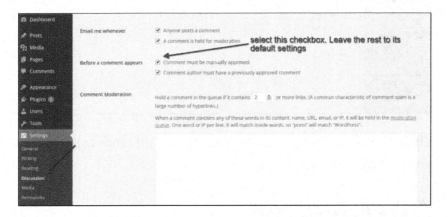

You can have a look at the other options as well. I recommend you leave the default values for now. When you're done click the *Save Changes* button at the bottom of the screen.

Finally, and most importantly, you need to make sure your website's pages have semantic URLs, that is, URLs humans and search engines can understand.

Access Settings -> Permalinks and choose your favourite URL structure from the following options:

- Day and name
- Month and name
- Post name

You have a few other options, but the three above are the most common and meaningful ones.

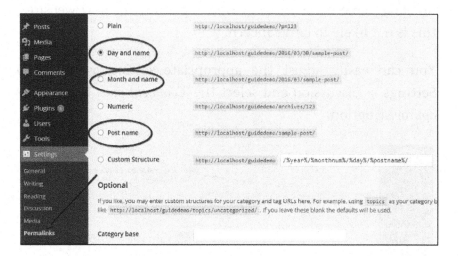

Click the *Save Changes* button to finish off and congratulate yourself on a job well done!

#4 Delete unused plugins

Unused plugins put your website at risk of getting hacked

To delete unused plugins go to Plugins -> Installed Plugins, select the plugin you want to delete and click the *Delete* link.

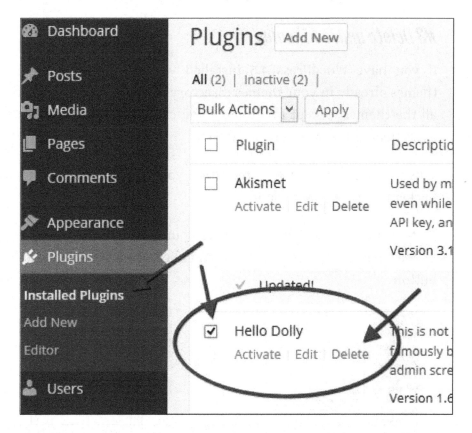

Confirm removal of the selected plugin on the following screen by clicking the 'Yes, delete these files' button and you're done!

WordPress comes with two default plugins: Akismet and Hello Dolly. Akismet is a great spam protection plugin, and you might want to use it before you launch your website. Hello Dolly is just a sample plugin which is there for sentimental reasons as part of the tradition of WordPress. It's definitely a plugin asking to be deleted.

#3 Delete unused themes

If you have WordPress 4.5 installed you should have three themes already in your themes directory. You need to get rid of all the themes, except for the one you choose to install and an extra default theme to use as fallback.

This is one more security precaution you need to take against hackers. Here's how to do it.

Go to Appearance -> Themes. Hover your mouse over the image of the theme you want to delete and click on the *Theme Details* button.

The next screen displays a *'Delete'* link at the bottom right. Hover over it and it now looks like a button. Click on it and confirm that you want to delete the theme. That's it!

I'm going to delete both the Twenty Fourteen and Twenty Fifteen themes, and keep Twenty Sixteen as my default theme. Later on, you're going to pick a theme for your website and Twenty Sixteen will be your fallback.

Conclusion

You've accomplished a lot in this chapter.

You've registered a domain name, purchased a hosting plan for your website, installed WordPress and performed a few configuration and clean up tasks.

Congratulations! Grab yourself a cup of coffee, take a break and come back to learn some more WordPress stuff.

CHAPTER 3:

Managing Content

WordPress is a blogging platform with full content management capabilities. In this chapter you're going to learn how to take control of your WordPress dashboard to create, edit, publish and delete awesome content to support your business goals.

Here's what you're going to do:

- learn what kind of content WordPress can handle and what this means for your business website
- how to create, edit, publish and delete blog Posts
- the best ways to manage comments
- how to manage Pages
- how to use the WordPress Media Library
- how to create, edit and delete navigation Menus
- how to add and remove WordPress Widgets

Let's begin!

48

3.1 What Kind of Content Can WordPress Handle?

Generally speaking, any piece of content you add to WordPress is a **Post**. However, to keep your stuff organized, WordPress natively handles different kinds of post. Here they are:

- Post
- Page
- Attachment
- Revisions
- Menus

In this chapter, you're going to learn about Posts, Pages and Menus. Attachments are usually files you attach to a post, like images, videos and audios, pdfs, etc. Revisions are something WordPress does automatically: as you write a post or a page and modify the content over time, WordPress keeps track of each modified version. This makes it very easy to go back to a previous draft if you change your mind about your work.

Developers can extend WordPress by adding custom content types, also called **custom post types**, to better meet websites' requirements. For instance, for a website that sells books or offers books reviews, organizing its entries into a *Book* content type rather than a *Post* content type certainly makes much more sense. Later in this guide you'll see how a number of popular plugins extend WordPress with their own custom post types.

Most first-time WordPress users find the difference between *posts* and *pages* a bit confusing. What's best for your content, a *post* or a *page*? Let's clarify things a bit.

49

When Do I Use a Post?

Your blog is made of posts. Here's what you need to know about posts:

- WordPress displays posts in reverse chronological order
- you can organize posts into categories and tags
- people can subscribe to your **RSS feed** to read your posts.

Think of posts as the news section of your website. Any time-sensitive information you'd like to share with your audience belongs to a post. For instance, stuff like the launch of your product, your view on some hot topic in your field, the latest project you did for a client, etc., are all great candidates for a blog post.

When do I Use a Page?

Despite looking like posts, pages have their distinctive features that make them better suited than posts for certain kinds of content. Pages

- are not listed by date and can't be categorized or tagged
- RSS readers don't have access to page content
- can be organized in hierarchical order, something like links in a dropdown menu where submenus are grouped under a parent menu item.

Use a WordPress page for fairly **static content** that's not going to change frequently over time. For instance, stuff about you and your business or information about how to get in touch with you, make much more sense displayed on a page than a post.

3.2 Creating, Editing, Publishing and Deleting Blog Posts

WordPress offers blogging capabilities out of the box, which means that creating and managing posts has never been easier.

But, you could be asking "I'm building a website for my business, do I really have to bother with a blog?". Adding a blog to your business website is one of the smartest moves you can do. Here's why.

Three Reasons Why Blogging is Great for Your Business

#1 Blogging helps drive more traffic to your website

Google loves fresh content on websites. Each new blog post means one more indexed page on your website. This increases your website's ranking on search engines results, which leads to more people finding your business online. Also, when you create a blog post, you're putting content online that people can share on social media, which helps expose your business to a new audience.

#2 Blogging helps generate new leads

Thanks to the engaging content that you put out there, your website now gets more traffic. What a good opportunity for you to convert that traffic into leads. Use strategically placed call to action buttons that offer visitors value in exchange for their email address. An ebook, a free webinar, a free trial or mini course are all great examples of lead generation call to actions. Having your visitors' email addresses is a powerful tool: you can start building a relationship with them by sending more valuable content their way as well as keeping them informed of your latest offer or awesome product.

#3 Blogging makes you an expert in your field

Lots of people go online to find answers to a problem. Find out the common problems your target audience is facing and write the answers they're looking for in a blog post. If people find helpful answers by visiting your blog, this increases their trust towards your business and your credibility as an expert in your field. People buy from people they trust, and this holds true for a brick and mortar business as much as , if not more, for an online business.

Now they I've hopefully convinced you of the goodness of blogging for your business, let's see how easily you can get started publishing those posts on WordPress.

How to Add a New Post

To add a new post you start by accessing the WordPress post editor from your WordPress dashboard. Follow these steps:

1. Locate the *Add New* submenu link under the *Posts* menu in the left-hand navigation of your Admin panel and click on it.

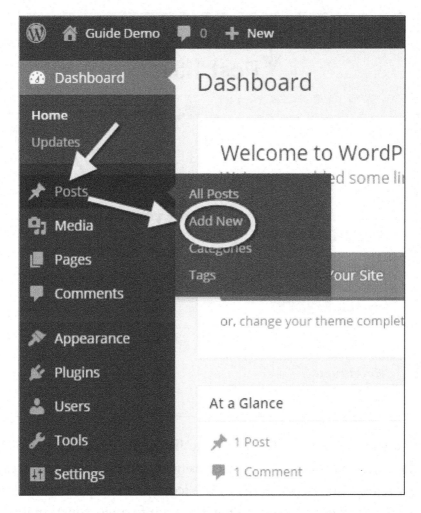

2. You're now on the Post editor screen. The WordPress text editor has a **Visual** tab and a **Text** tab.

The Visual tab with its intuitive and user-friendly interface is active by default. It allows you to use the editor pretty much the same way you would use a common word processor.

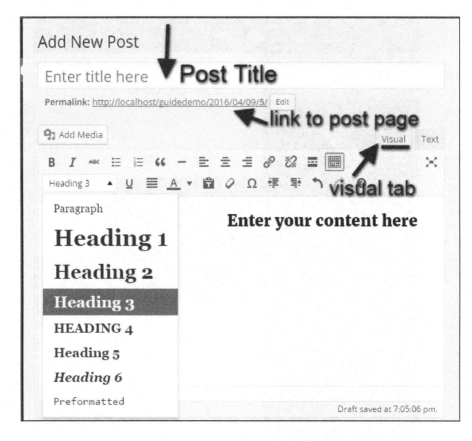

You start by writing the post title in the textbox at the top of the page and the rest of your content inside the main text area. If you don't know what any of the icons at the top of the editor is for, hover over it and you'll get some info on its functionality.

The Text tab lets you enter HTML content. For those who are not scared of HTML, this is the best way to get full control of the formatting of your post.

Irrespective of using the Visual or the Text screen, try to break down your post into **headings, paragraphs** and **bulleted lists.** This helps your website visitors scan and read what you write and engage with your post.

Also, avoid changing the font style and colours in the editor. **Let your theme control the appearance** of your website. This ensures that the look and feel of your website stays consistent and professional.

You've written your post, what next?

Once you're happy with your post perhaps you're tempted to hit Publish. Hold on, your content requires some extra touches to make it more searchable to both humans and search engines.

How to categorize and tag your blog posts

With WordPress you can associate a post with one or more **categories**. You can create categories in two ways:

- From the *Categories* panel.
- On the Post editor page when adding or editing your post.

You get to the *Categories* panel from the *Categories* submenu inside the *Post* menu of the dashboard's main navigation:

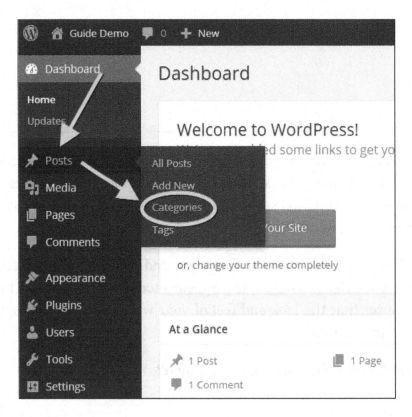

Once you're on the *Categories* panel, you have the option to manage existing categories on the right-hand pane or to add a new category on the left-hand pane:

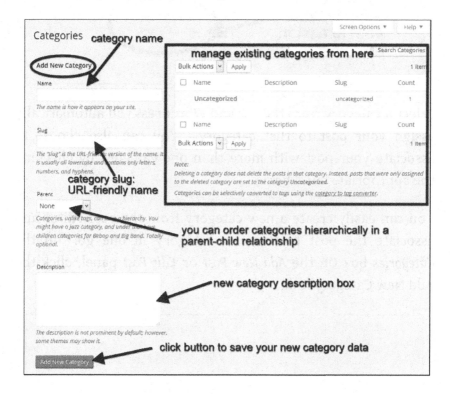

To add a new category, simply fill out the form and click the *Add New Category* button at the bottom. If at any point you're unsure about the information required, read the hint at the bottom of each form field for a friendly explanation.

Once you have the category available, it's easy to assign it to your post either at the time you create the post or when you're in the process of editing it.

Try it yourself. Go to the *Add New Post* page and locate the *Categories* box on the right-hand side

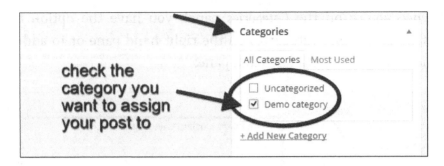

Select a category from the list and WordPress will automatically assign your post to that category. You can also choose to associate your post with more than one category by checking the appropriate checkboxes.

You can easily create a new category from the post editor and associate the post to the new category in one go. In the *Categories* box On the *Add New Post* or *Edit Post* panel, click the Add New Category link:

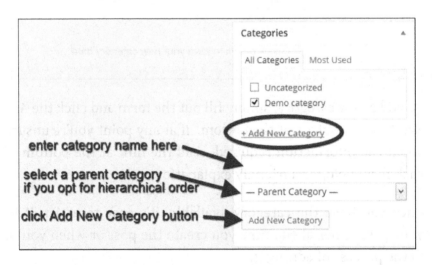

A sub-panel slides open where you can enter the category name, optionally assign a parent category if you're creating a sub-category (e.g., category: *Books*, sub-category: *Science Fiction*), and click the *Add New Category* button.

Tags work in a similar way to Categories. You'll find the *Tags* box below the *Categories* box in the right-hand pane of the *Post* editor screen.

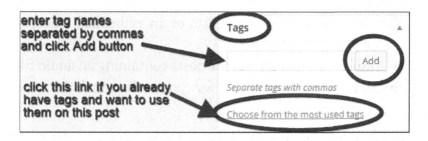

Just add your tags separated by commas and click the *Add* button. For example, if your post is under the *Fitness* category and you write about dieting, you can enter - *eating, diet, mediterranean diet* - in the *Tags* textbox.

Categorizing and tagging your posts is very important both as a way of giving structure and organization to your blog and to help people and Google crawlers find your content.

Post formats

Posts formats can be a bit confusing. These are an optional feature to style your posts differently according to the way your post presents its content. Here's the list of post formats WordPress makes available:

- **Standard** - this is the default post format
- **Aside** - something like a note, usually styled without title
- **Gallery** - use this format if your post displays a gallery of images

- **Link** - for posts that only contain a single link to another website or resource, you can use this format
- **Image** - this format is for posts that display a single image
- **Quote** - if your post contains just a quotation, a *quote* post format can display it in an attractive way
- **Status** - this format is for short Twitter-like status updates
- **Video** - if your post consists of an embedded video, you can give it this format
- **Audio** - use this format for posts containing an audio file
- **Chat** - This format is for posts that include a chat transcript.

These formats are only there to give your content a distinctive appearance that better enhances the kind of content in your post. For instance, if you post a YouTube video and assign the Video post format to it, your theme can display your video post with a nice video icon close to the title, or in a different color. It's all about giving appropriate visual cues to your blog visitors about the format you've chosen for your content in the post.

You don't have to apply a post format, and not all themes support them. **Some themes offer no support for post formats** while others offer support only for a few of them. If your theme supports post formats, you should see them listed on the right-hand pane of the *Post* editor page, above the *Categories* box.

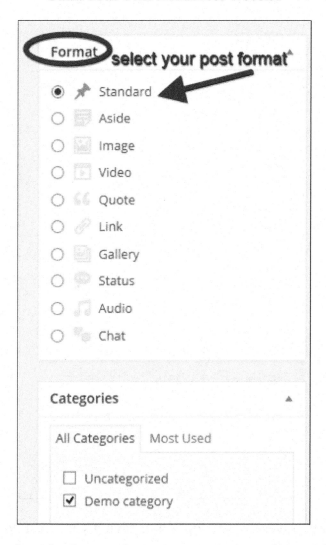

Simply select the format that suits your content best and you're done!

Different options of saving and publishing your post

You'll find the *Publish* box on the top left of the Post editor screen.

WordPress gives you the option of saving your post as *Draft* or *Pending Review*.

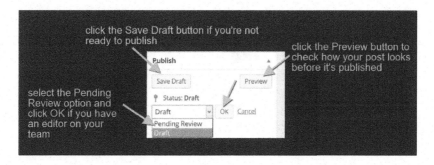

You save your post as *Draft* if you're not ready to share it on the Internet. Let's say, you're not totally happy with it and would like to revise it, or you haven't finished writing it and would like to pick it up later.

If you have an Editor on your team who reviews your articles before they go live, then saving your post with a status of *Pending Review* makes sense.

Before publishing your post, it's a good idea to make sure it's formatted as expected and looks good. Just click the *Preview* button and check your work.

You can also control the **visibility** of a published post. You can choose to have your post:

- **Public** - anyone can access it
- **Password-protected** - only visitors with the correct password can access it
- **Private** - no one can access it.

The *Public* option gives you the choice to mark your post as **sticky**.

A sticky post is always displayed at the top of the posts lists, no matter how many posts you publish after that. Use this option when you want your visitors to have easy access to specific posts at all times.

Now hit that *Publish* button and congratulate yourself: your first blog post is in the wild.

Editing your blog post

You can change your post at any time both while it's still in draft format and after it's been published. Here's what you need to do.

- From the main Dashboard menu on the left, go to *Posts -> All Posts*
- Hover over the post you want to edit and click the *Edit* or *Quick Edit* button.

If you only need to change stuff like title, categories, tags, etc., without touching text or images, then click the *Quick Edit* button and a panel slides down where you can make your changes.

However, to change text or images, you need to click on the *Edit* button, which lands you on the post editor screen. Make your mods and click *Update.*

Deleting posts

If you change your mind about a post and want to remove it altogether, WordPress makes this very easy to do.

Go ahead and delete the *Hello World* post WordPress adds by default. By the way, I recommend you **delete all types of default content you find in your WordPress installation**. This is good practice and prevents having that cheesy content indexed by search engines by mistake.

In the *All Posts* panel, hover over the post you want to delete and click on the *Trash* link.

Next, click on the *Trash* tab.

Finally, hover over the post you want to remove and click on the *Delete Permanently* link. You can also select the checkbox next to your post and click on the *Empty Trash* button on the top right of the screen.

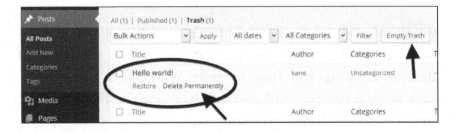

And that's it, you got rid of the unwanted post.

Where to find help

If you're stuck at any time, help is at hand.

In the Post Editor screen, you'll find a *Help* button on the top right of the page.

Clicking the button shows a sliding panel with tons of information on how to perform the most common tasks relating to adding and editing posts.

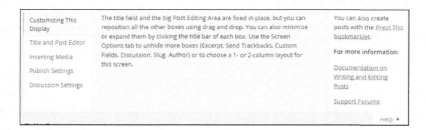

3.3 Managing Comments

One of the great things about running your own blog is getting to know and engaging with your readers.

By default, WordPress displays a comment box at the bottom of each single post page. If your readers have already left comments, WordPress displays them in a list.

You can manage comments in a similar way to how you manage posts.

Access the *Comments* screen from the Dashboard main menu:

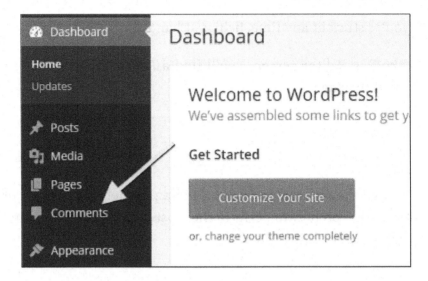

The *Comments* screen is very intuitive.

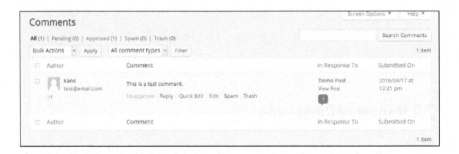

Hover your mouse on the comment text and the following links appear:

- Approve/Unapprove
- Reply
- Quick Edit
- Edit
- Spam
- Trash

You click on each of them to accomplish the desired task.

The sub-navigation related to the comments lets you browse comments on the basis of the following filters:

- All (default screen)
- Pending
- Approved
- Spam
- Trash

Comments in the *Trash* folder can be restored to where they were before being trashed (either in the *Pending* or *Approved* folder), but they can also be marked as spam, or permanently deleted. Just click on the appropriate link.

Comments in the *Spam* folder can be either marked as *Not Spam*, let's say you've changed your mind or realized the comment was perfectly legitimate after all, or permanently deleted.

You can also manage your comments one at a time or in bulk from the *Bulk Actions* dropdown box.

For instance, here's how you approve a couple of comments in the *Pending* folder.

First, select the comments you want to manage. If you select the checkbox at the top of the screen next to the *Author* link, you'll automatically select all comments available on that panel.

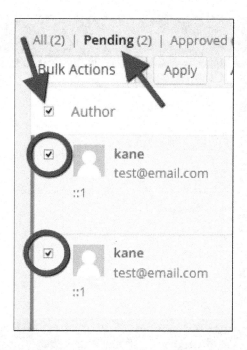

Next, select the action you want to perform from the dropdown box on the left, in this case select *Approve,* and click the *Apply* button.

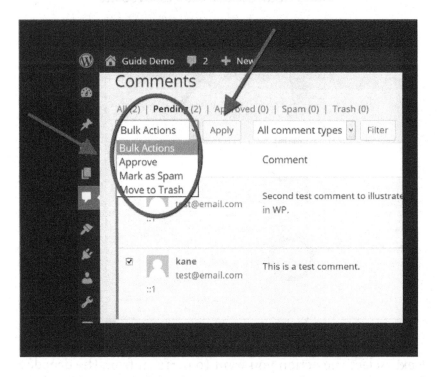

Great, you've moved both comments to the *Approved* panel. Check it out!

How you can have more control on comments

You can also make site-wide decisions about things like how many comments to show per page, how many levels to display in threaded comments (if your theme supports threaded comments), the order you'd like your comments to be displayed, who can leave comments on your website, etc.

Simply access the *Discussion* panel from the Settings menu in the Dashboard.

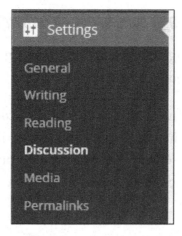

Select your options on the *Discussion Settings* screen and click the *Save Changes* button at the bottom of the page.

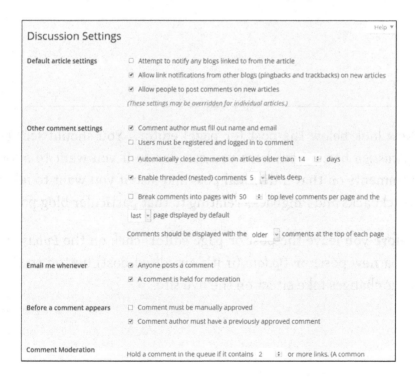

How you can manage comments on individual posts

You can also manage comments at a more granular level inside individual posts and pages.

For instance, open one post in the editor and access the *Discussion* settings inside the editor's panel. If you can't see the *Discussion* settings, click the *Screen Options* button at the top of the screen and select the *Discussion* checkbox.

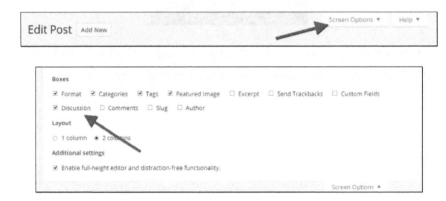

Now look below the post (or page) editor. You should see the *Discussion* box. From here you can decide if you want to allow comments on that individual post and also if you want to allow Trackbacks and Pingbacks relating to that particular blog post.

Before you leave the post or page editor, click on the *Publish* (if it's a new post) or *Update* (if it's an edited post) button so that your changes take effect on the live site.

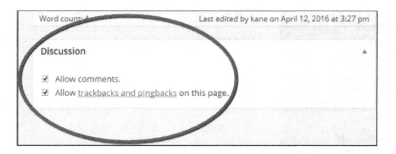

If you're wondering what on earth trackbacks and pingbacks are, here's a short explanation from the **Codex** website, where users and developers find most of the knowledge about WordPress.

Trackbacks are ways to "notify another author that you wrote something related to what he had written on his blog, even if you don't have an explicit link to his article."

Pingbacks are ways in which you can "notify the author of an article if you link to his article (article on a blog, of course)".

Try to schedule some time in your day to answer comments and engage with your visitors. This will go a long way to building your audience and establishing trust with them. Enjoy!

3.4 Managing Pages

You manage Pages in WordPress in a way similar to managing Posts. There are some differences, however, which is what I'm mostly going to focus on in this section.

You access the *Pages* panel from the *Pages* menu in the Dashboard. From there you can edit, trash, delete, and view pages, either individually or in bulk.

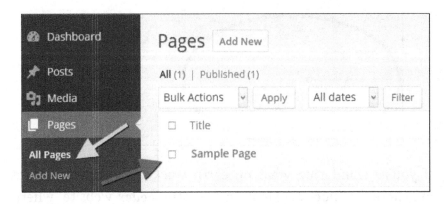

Have a go at deleting the *Sample Page* WordPress creates by default and try adding a new page. You can access the Page editor from the *Add New* link, just below the *All Pages* link.

One significant difference between a post and a page is that you can't categorize or tag a page.

However, you can order pages in hierarchical order by placing one page as child of a parent page. Think of this relation in terms of the relation between a main menu link and a submenu link in a dropdown menu.

You can order pages from the *Page Attributes* box on the right of the Page editor screen.

To demonstrate how this works, add a couple of pages to your website. Open the second page in the Page editor and locate the *Page Attributes* box.

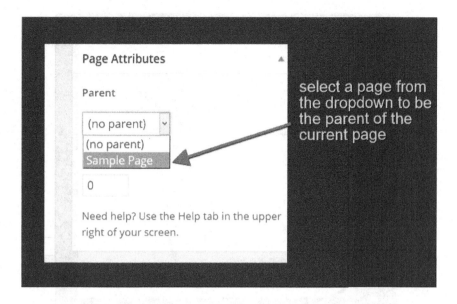

Select the parent page and click the *Publish* button if you're just creating the page or the *Update* button if you're working on an existing page.

If your theme has different page templates for different layouts, e.g., a Homepage template, a full-width template, etc., they would be listed in the *Page Attributes* box.

To show how this works, I'm going to use the Twenty Fourteen theme, which offers a number of custom templates. If I access any of the pages from the editor panel, I see a *Templates* dropdown box inside the *Page Attributes* section of the screen. I select the *Full Width Page* template from the list and hit *Update*. Now that particular page will have a different look and feel from the others, courtesy of the custom template the theme developers provided for us.

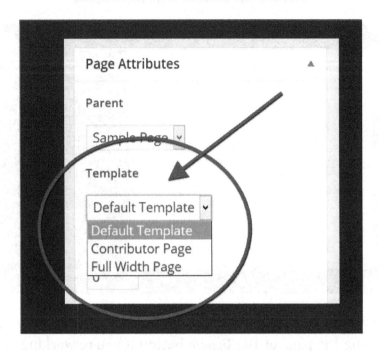

Now you know all you need to start adding and managing pages in your website. You can order pages hierarchically and apply custom templates to give them a unique look and feel.

3.5 How to Use the WordPress Media Library

The Media Library is where WordPress stores the media files you upload to your website. You can upload images, video files, audio files, pdf files, etc., and manage them all from there.

To access the Media Library, expand the *Media* menu from the WordPress Dashboard.

To add a new media item to your library, click the *Add New* link. From here, upload a new image. You can do so either by dropping the image file into the dot-bordered box or by clicking the *Select Files* button. This allows you to browse to the location where your media file is stored on your computer and upload it to your site.

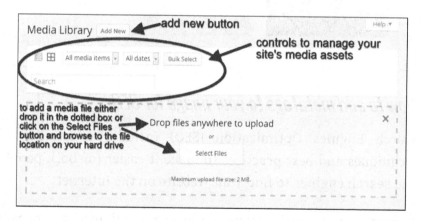

Once your asset has been uploaded, you can see it on display in the library panel. Here's the Media Library in my WordPress dashboard after I've just uploaded two images.

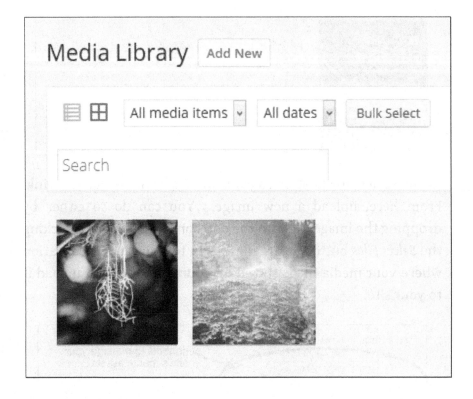

How to add metatags to your image for SEO

Search Engines Optimization (SEO) includes a number of techniques and best practices to make it easier for both people and search engines to find your website on the Internet.

Adding some information to the images' markup is a core SEO best practice as well as accessibility requirement. The all-important information is called **Alt Text**, which is alternative text that makes the content of your image accessible to people with sight impairments as well as search engine crawlers. Additional info you can add is an image description, a title, and an image caption.

Adding this info from the Media Library is simple.

Click on the image in the Media Library to access the *Attachment Details* screen. You can fill out the textboxes to your right with the desired information and you're done!

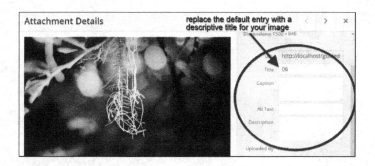

Make sure you **Title, Caption, Alt Text** (the most important bit), and **Description** describe your image. Also, throw in one or two keywords for good measure, as long as they relate to your image.

How to edit your images in the WordPress Media Library

The WordPress Media Library lets you edit your images, so your website can have gorgeous graphics without the need for an expensive image editing software like Photoshop.

Here's what you need to do.

Click on the image, then click on the *Edit Image* button.

From here you can crop, rotate, flip or scale your image.

Try playing with the controls available in the panel and check the result. When you're happy with your image click the *Save* button.

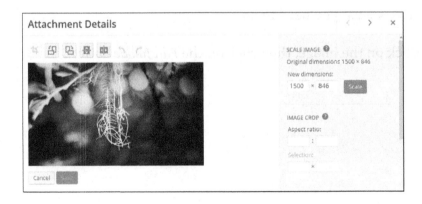

It's important to know that very large images slow down your website, which is going to have a negative impact on your website's Google ranking. However, low quality images make your website look unprofessional. Try to **strike the right balance between your images quality and their filesize.** Here's a secret: **look for the recommended image size in your theme's documentation and crop your images accordingly.**

Inserting images in posts and pages

You can add images to your posts and pages by selecting them from what's already available in the Media Library. If you need to upload an image, you can do so from the Post or Page editor. Doing so will store the image in the Media Library and display it in your post or page at the same time.

Try adding an image to one of your posts.

First, open your selected post in the Editor screen and place the cursor where you want the image to be displayed.

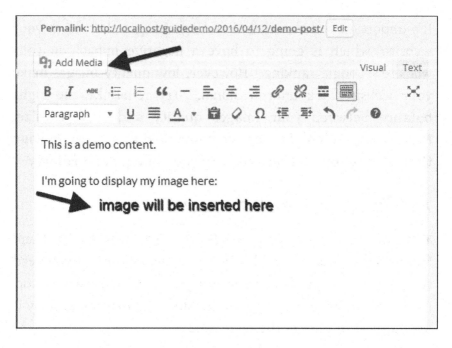

WordPress opens a panel that gives you a few media options.

You can:

- upload an image by dropping it into the screen
- select an image already available in the Media Library by clicking the *Insert Media* link
- create an image gallery
- insert a featured image
- upload an image from the Internet by entering its location's URL.

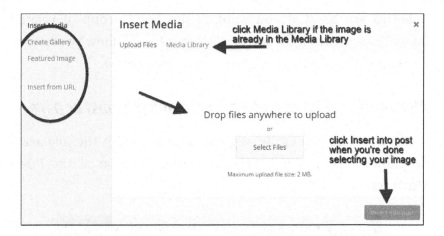

What is a featured image? Here's how WordPress.com defines featured images:

> "A featured image represent the contents, mood, or *theme of a post or page. Posts and pages can have a single featured image, which many themes and tools can use to enhance the presentation of your site.*"

Most themes support featured images, and if your theme is among them, you'll also have the opportunity to upload a featured image from the *Featured Image* box to the right of the Post or Page editor.

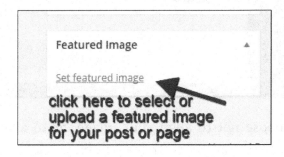

Galleries are great if you want to display a group of related images in a meaningful and attractive way. I'll show you how to create a gallery in WordPress in the section below.

More options before adding your image to a post or page

WordPress lets you easily align your image from the *Alignment* dropdown box in the *Attachment Settings* section of the *Insert Media* screen.

You can choose not to align your image, or to align it to the **right, left,** or **center**. I find that small images look best aligned to the left or right, while medium to large images are best displayed aligned to the center.

You can also choose to link your image to:

- the **Media File** - clicking on the image will display the full image in the browser
- an **Attachment Page** - if your theme has an `image.php` or `attachment.php` template file, the image will be linked to the page controlled by either of these templates. If not, it will display the same as any regular single post page
- a **Custom URL** - you can choose to link your image anywhere on the Internet.

Finally, you can decide the size for your image. You can choose from the **thumbnail**, **medium**, **large** and **full size** options in the dropdown box.

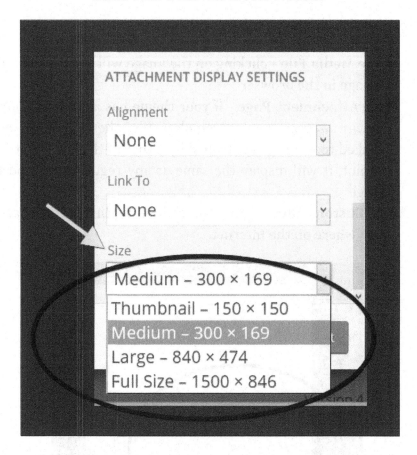

When you're finished selecting your image, click the *Insert into post* link. Now the image you've just selected should be displayed exactly where you wanted.

Well done!

How to create a WordPress gallery

There are tons of plugins out there that let you add all sorts of fancy galleries and sliders. However, if your theme makes the native gallery look attractive enough, my motto is: go with what you already have and add plugins only if necessary.

These are the steps to set up a native WordPress image gallery.

First, upload a few images. What's a gallery for if you don't have images to show off? Click the *Add Media* button from the post editor and drop a few images on the *Insert Media* screen.

Next, click the *Create Gallery* button

Now, select the images for your gallery. Simply click on each image and WordPress marks it as selected. You'll also see thumbnails of the selected images at the bottom of the panel. If you want to deselect any of the images, hover over the tick icon and you'll see it metamorphose into a minus sign. Click the minus sign to remove that image from your selection.

Once you're done, click the *Create a new gallery* button.

Now you're on the *Edit Gallery* panel, which gives you a few options.

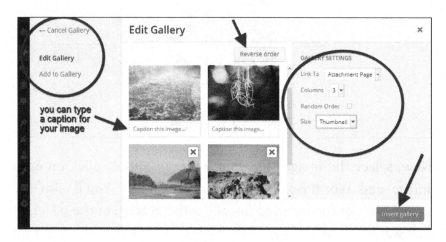

To the left, you find buttons to cancel the gallery or add more images to it.

In the middle, you have options to reverse the order of the images by clicking the *Reverse order* button or simply dragging the images with your mouse. You can also add captions to each image to make it clearer to your visitors what the image is about.

To the right of the panel, you can choose to add links to your images, number of columns, decide image size (thumbnail, medium, large or full size). I find that thumbnails look better on a three-column gallery and medium images work best on two-column galleries.

You can also choose to display your images randomly by selecting the *Random Order* checkbox.

When you're finished, go ahead and click the *Insert gallery* button. You should now see the gallery in your editor. To check how the gallery is displayed on your website before it goes live, click the *Preview Changes* button.

This is what my gallery looks like using the Twenty Sixteen default theme.

This is my caption

Not bad!

If you're happy with your gallery, click on *Update* to save your changes and enjoy.

You can edit your gallery at any time. If you click anywhere on the gallery inside your Post or Page editor, two icons pop up, one to edit the gallery and one to delete it.

That's it, your website can now show off your best pics in a nice gallery display.

3.6 Creating, editing and Deleting Navigation Menus

Navigation is the most important component in your website. Place it in an obvious place, preferably at the top of the page and make sure it's fully accessible both using the mouse and the keyboard.

WordPress gives you everything you need to create navigation menus, it's your theme's job to display and style them.

Here's how you create your main navigation menu.

First, access the *Menus* panel in your WordPress dashboard.

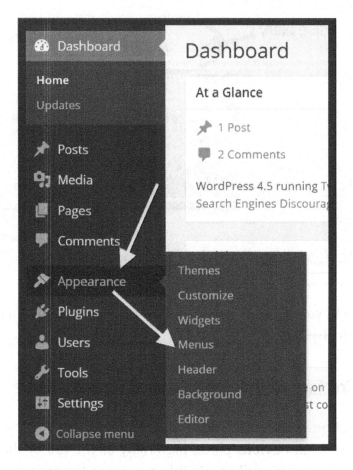

Once you're on the *Menus* screen, pick a name for your menu and type it in the appropriate textbox. I've called my menu *Main Menu* to make it clear that it represents the website's main navigation. Then, click the *Create Menu* button.

The next step is to assign a location to your menu. Your theme makes available one or more places where you can display a menu. You can see how many menus your theme supports and where they will be displayed on your website in the *Menu Settings* section of the *Menus* panel. Here, you'll find the Theme locations sub-section, which in the Twenty Sixteen theme looks like this.

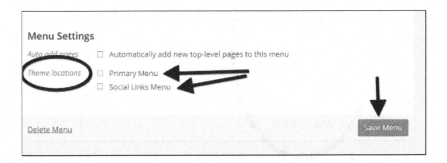

If you're following along with the same theme, select the *Primary Menu* checkbox for your theme location. This ensures your navigation will display properly on the website. Then click the *Save Menu* button.

Next, you add pages to your menu and decide on its structure. Is it going to be a one-level navigation menu or is it going to include submenus? My recommendation is to keep the structure simple and logical, so your visitors won't find it confusing.

You add menu items using the options available from the left side of the *Menus* screen. From there you can:

- add one or more pages (select the checkbox next to the page title and click on the *Add to Menu* button)
- add one or more posts (select the checkbox next to the post title and click on the *Add to Menu* button
- add one or more custom links. This option is especially useful if you want to add a menu item that links to an external website or resource
- add one or more categories (select the checkbox next to the category name and click the *Add to Menu* button).

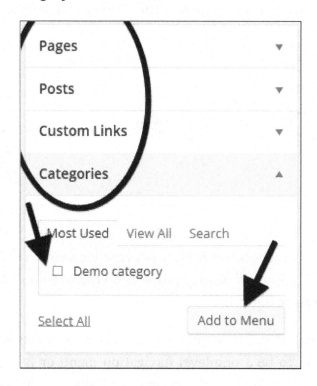

As you make your selections and add items to your menu, these will appear in the *Menu Structure* section to the right. From there you can reorder your menu items or build submenu items just by dragging and dropping each link.

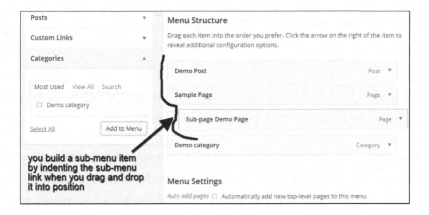

Be warned: doing so only builds the structure of your navigation. Whether or not the dropdown structure is displayed on the website depends on your theme. If your theme provides styles for dropdown menus, or hierarchical menus, then your desired structure will appear on the live website.

Once you're happy with your menu, click the *Save Menu* button and check the result.

Here's what my menu looks like on the Twenty Sixteen theme.

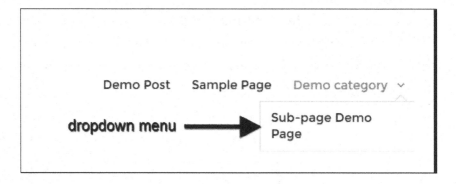

All looks fine. When I hover over the Demo Category item, the dropdown submenu link pops up as expected.

Try out your navigation on a mobile screen and make sure you can access all its menu items. Most modern themes should be mobile-ready, and having users struggle with your navigation on their tiny devices is the last thing you want.

Here's what the mobile navigation menu looks like in the Twenty Sixteen theme.

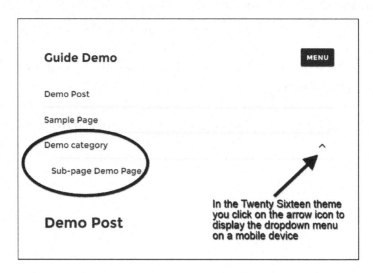

The right theme must let your users easily navigate your website both on desktop and mobile.

3.7 How to Add and Remove Widgets

WordPress widgets are tools that make available some kind of functionality specific to your website. Some widgets come bundled with WordPress by default, e.g., *Calendar*, *Recent Comments*, *Recent Posts*, and many more, including the simplest yet in my view the most versatile of all, the *Text* widget. This lets you embed simple text content as well as HTML markup, which is great if you want to add your own block of custom text and style it any way you like.

You access the *Widgets* panel from the main Dashboard menu via *Appearance -> Widgets*.

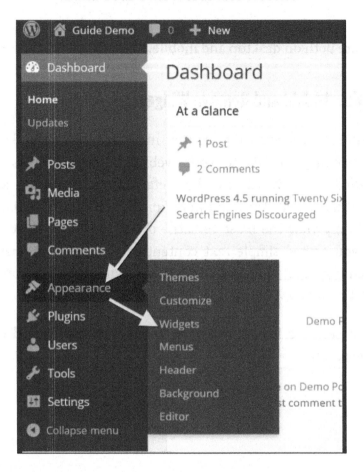

It's your theme that selects which areas of your website, called **dynamic sidebars** or **widget-ready areas,** can display widgets. You can easily find out how many sidebars your theme supports and where they are located in the website layout from the right-hand pane of the *Widgets* screen.

Build Your Own WordPress Website

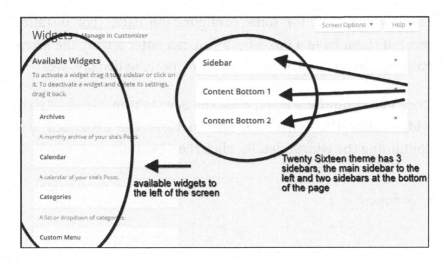

On the left you'll find all the widgets available to your website. Some themes and plugins provide additional widgets with specific functionality like sliders, subscription forms, etc.

Adding a widget to a sidebar is a breeze.

Just expand the sidebar where you want your widget to be displayed, if it's not already expanded. Next, drag and drop your selected widget into the sidebar.

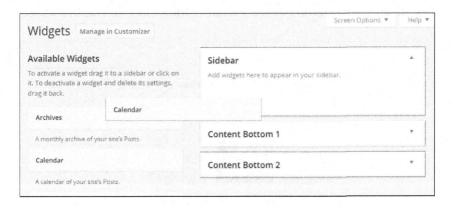

101

Some widgets ask for some configuration data. For instance, most of them have a box where you can enter a title, the *Recent Posts* widget lets you decide how many posts to display, etc.

Once you drop the widget, click the *Save* button. To delete the widget click the *Delete* link and to close the expanded area containing the widget details, click the *Close* link.

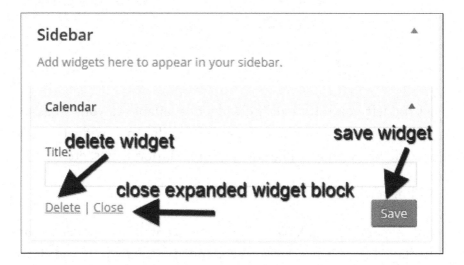

I've just added the *Calendar* widget to the Twenty Sixteen theme's main sidebar. Here's what it looks like in the browser.

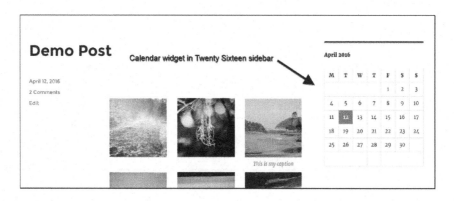

Sidebars are a great way to add small functional bits to your website quickly and easily. Make sure your theme supports at least one sidebar. In my view, the more the better, but I'm getting ahead of myself - the next chapter is all about themes.

Conclusion

This has been a super long chapter, but going through it and experimenting with the content management capabilities of WordPress is a crucial step to start using this great platform.

You now know

- when to use a post or it's more appropriate to use a page
- how to create, edit, publish and delete posts and pages
- how to manage users' comments
- how to use the WordPress Media Library
- how to create and manage navigation menus
- how to add, configure and delete widgets.

Great job! Take a break and I'll see you in the next chapter where you can start learning some awesome stuff about WordPress themes.

CHAPTER 4:

Design & Layout

WordPress themes control the look and feel of your website. The initial impact your website makes on your visitors is crucial in conveying professionalism and trust. It's your chosen theme's job to deliver that all-important first impression.

Here's what you're going to learn in this chapter:

- how to choose a great WordPress theme for your website's goals
- how to install and activate your chosen WordPress theme
- how to configure your WordPress theme
- how to customize your WordPress theme

Time to dive in!

4.1 How to Choose a WordPress Theme

The vast amount of WordPress themes you can find online is astounding, but this often means that choosing the right theme for your website can be more, not less, overwhelming.

Should You Go for a Free or Paid Theme?

You'll find that WordPress themes are distributed on the basis of the following models:

- **free themes** - like WordPress itself, these themes are GPL-licensed. You can also find places where themes are distributed under one of the Creative Commons license flavours
- **freemium themes** - these are themes offering a limited number of features for free, usually as a way of promoting the paid version of the same theme but boasting a wider set of features
- paid themes – Personally we recommend, themeforest. They have great support, our theme id s purchased from them and they have huge amounts of themes available. These themes are offered at a price, either for the standalone theme or as part of a membership package. Expect to pay anything between $50 and $200 for a WordPress theme from well-established vendors.

Until not very long ago, you could make the argument that paid themes were better on the grounds that a number of free themes were poorly coded, didn't have attractive modern designs, and could even hide malicious code and spammy links.

Nowadays, if you take care to download your free theme from a reputable source, this is not the case. You'll find an increasing number of well coded, safe and attractive, premium quality free WordPress themes.

This situation isn't of much help to the average WordPress user who needs some criteria to discriminate between the various offers available.

To alleviate some of the difficulties you might have when making your choice, I'll give you a few pointers before you commit to any of the theme distribution models I outlined above.

What's great about free themes

No price tag attached

Free themes are ... free, no need to open your wallet before you can go ahead with the download. However, you'd better read the license terms because some theme authors use different license terms for different assets included in the theme, or for support. For instance, you can find that you can use and modify the theme, but not the images that come with it. In some cases, you can use the theme for free, but need to keep an attribution link that acknowledges the theme's author. Again, there are circumstances when the theme is free, but not updates or support. Just *read the small print.*

Fewer bells and whistles

It's likely that free themes come with fewer features and embellishments in comparison with some paid themes. I consider this a plus. Simple, lightweight themes are often (alas not always) easier to use, fast-loading, and less distracting for your website visitors.

Freedom to experiment

It often happens that you've checked out the theme's live demo, you love the theme, but when you add your content to it, things don't look quite as you expected. With a free theme, it's a breeze to just try out as many themes as you like until you find the one that best suits your website content, goals and brand. This can be ridiculously expensive if you're buying themes at $50 or so a pop.

What's not so great about free themes

Lack of originality

The Internet bursts with blogs offering curated lists of best free WordPress themes. These themes become quickly popular and get hundreds, even thousands, of downloads in a short amount of time. If uniqueness and originality are your thing, going for a free theme can make your quest for the right one way more difficult and time consuming.

Help is not always available

While with a paid theme support is almost always a given, free WordPress themes don't often come with guaranteed support. It's true, you can post a cry for help on the WordPress.org forums and wait for some generous volunteer or the theme's author to answer. However, you can never be sure help will be forthcoming. With themeforest for example, the envato team are there to help 24/7.

Updates can be hard to come by

WordPress development is mind-blowingly fast. New versions have been coming up sometimes within just a few months apart from each other. Ensuring that a theme is compatible with the latest WordPress release, fixing bugs, coding patches, etc., are time consuming tasks and often authors of free themes are not under any clear obligation to provide this level of support for their product.

Before leaving the topic of free WordPress themes, I need to stress this crucial point:

Where you download your free WordPress theme is of the utmost importance. The safest place is the WordPress.org themes repository, where each theme is carefully reviewed before being accepted. Also, there are some reputable WordPress themes companies, which often have free themes available for download. Especially if you're not familiar with good code and WordPress coding standards, it's **better if you stay away from unknown websites offering free themes for download** - you never know what you let yourself in for.

What's great about paid themes

Regular updates

Paid themes by established and reputable developers/companies have powerful business incentives and obligations to their customer base to keep their product up-to-date with each new release of WordPress.

This constitutes an added layer of peace of mind for you.

More uniqueness in the design

It's easier to browse paid themes and find something that's not been downloaded thousands of times. This increases the chances that your website won't have much of the cookie-cutter template look and feel.

Theme documentation

It's pretty standard for paid themes to include detailed documentation. This can be a PDF document, tutorial videos, tutorial articles, etc. I'm not saying free themes don't offer this all-important feature, just that it's not always there, and when it's there it's not always as thorough as it should be.

Ongoing support

Paid themes usually offer various avenues of support, e.g., live chat, email ticketing system, forum, etc. Free themes usually offer limited support.

This means that if you're stuck when you're customizing your paid theme, you're most likely to find help on the company's website.

What's not so great about paid themes

The price

As a business owner, you can see the price for a WordPress theme as either a cost or an investment. I tend to view a solid and well supported theme from a great company as more of an investment, especially if you're not an expert coder or not willing to become one.

More options to configure

Most premium themes ship with their own custom administration panel crammed with tons of customization settings. While this gives you more freedom to add your modifications without touching a line of code, learning all the settings and experimenting with them can absorb quite a bit of your time.

Code bloat

Paid themes tend to include a lot of bells and whistles. I'm talking about those themes advertising multiple sliders, portfolio functionality, twenty + page layouts and styles, hundreds of shortcodes, etc. A number of users may think a theme like this lets them create any website they like without any code. However, this is not always the case: if you require serious customizations, you'll still need a professional on board. Also, it's unlikely you'll need all the features the theme offers, and what you don't use will only make your website slower and even more vulnerable (think of all those sliders that need some updating from time to time). Finally, the so-called 'kitchen sink' theme can reserve you some nasty surprises when you eventually decide to change theme. In fact, when a substantial amount of your content is being generated by the theme's shortcodes or custom settings, once you change theme that content won't be available on your website. **Beware of theme lock-in.**

General Consideration When Choosing Your Theme

I'm going to mention some guidelines to help you choose the WordPress theme that best suits your business goals for your website. These apply both to free and paid themes.

Focus your choice by defining your needs

With all the amazing-looking themes out there, it's easy to fall into the trap of going for the prettiest theme, or the theme that has that trendy parallax effect you see on every other website, or the theme that has those snazzy animation effects that look so modern, and so on and so forth.

This is not the way to go. What you need before you start on your quest is a plan. What are the most important aspects of your site? To figure this out, here are a few questions you need to ask yourself.

Is your website going to be content-heavy or a small, brochure website?

As a small business owner, your site is likely to be something in between. Your website will have to show prospective clients what you have to offer, your **unique selling proposition** (what differentiates you from the competition), testimonials, latest news from the blog, etc. However, you don't need to overwhelm visitors with pages and pages of text. So readability and easy, intuitive navigation are crucial. Also, it's likely you won't need an animation-heavy website, which will at best distract your customers from what you want them to do on the web page, at worst too much moving stuff can be annoying and even have adverse effects on visitors with certain health conditions.

What about e-commerce?

Do you plan on selling any products or services from your website? As we're discussing how to build a small business website, this is probably the case. The best e-commerce plugin for WordPress at the time of writing is WooCommerce, therefore a WooCommerce-enabled theme will make setting up shop much quicker and easier.

What do you think will be the most important stuff to display on your website's homepage?

Browse your competition's websites. Jot down what you think works and doesn't work. This will give you some concrete features to look for when selecting your theme, not just in light of what looks nice but also in terms of what benefit a specific feature brings to the table for your business.

The important point to keep in mind is that most themes are not one-size-fits-all. Having a good idea of what your site needs is the biggest factor in choosing the theme that's right for your business.

Choose a MOBILE-FRIENDLY theme

Nowadays websites need to be responsive. This means that they adjust their layout across different screen sizes and devices.

If you don't want to risk alienating potential clients accessing your website from mobile devices or being penalized by Google, make sure your theme looks good and is usable on tablet and mobile devices. The easiest way to do the test is by visiting the theme's live demo site (if a theme doesn't have one it's probably not worth your time or your money) and resizing your browser screen. The theme's layout should smoothly flow with the screen, the content should be easily readable, horizontal scrollbars should not be visible, and you should be able to use the navigation without any problems.

If you want to push your testing further, copy the URL of the theme's demo page and paste it in Google's Mobile Friendly Test page.

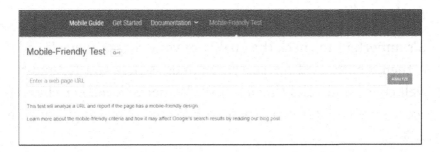

Testing for different browsers

Visitors will be coming to your website using a wide range of browsers. I recommend you test your selected theme's demo site on as many browsers as you can get your hands on, both on desktop and mobile. At least, make sure you test on the latest versions of:

- Internet Explorer
- Microsoft Edge (latest Microsoft browser running on Windows 10)
- Mozilla Firefox

- Chrome
- Opera
- Safari

Support

Check out the kind of support available for your chosen theme before committing to it. It doesn't matter how many times the theme's promo page says how easy it is to customize the theme in any way you like without code. The reality is, you can get stuck, and when it happens, you need to know where you can go for help.

Code quality

It's important to check the quality of your chosen theme's code. A theme optimized for search engines is first and foremost a well coded and valid theme. If you're not a developer chances are it's not easy for you to assess code quality by simply looking at it.

Don't despair, there are tools out there that give you some indication of the quality of your theme's code. The first port of call should be the W3C Markup Validation Service website, an online service that tests the validity of HTML code.

Simply enter your theme's demo site URL in the input box and click the *Check* button. The service spits out all the code that doesn't comply with HTML coding standards. Just look out for serious errors, but don't pay too much attention to the warnings.

There are tests you can perform after you download the theme. I admit, these are more useful when you download free themes than paid themes. In fact, if there's stuff wrong with the free theme you can just discard it and move on, while doing so with paid themes can become a bit expensive.

You can verify that your theme doesn't hide any malicious code, or that it doesn't have PHP or other code-related errors, by uploading the theme's ZIP file to the Theme Check online service.

As a final recommendation, **it's always a good idea to check users ratings and reviews** for any theme you're about to download or buy. They're a fairly reliable indicator of how easy it is to use the theme, the level of support for the theme and its overall quality.

4.2 Installing a WordPress Theme

You can download a theme from WordPress.org or from a marketplace. Let's look into each of these possibilities in turn.

Installing your theme from WordPress.org

If your theme is hosted on WordPress.org, you can quickly download it from the WordPress dashboard by following these steps.

Access the *Themes* panel from *Appearance* -> *Themes* in your WordPress dashboard main menu.

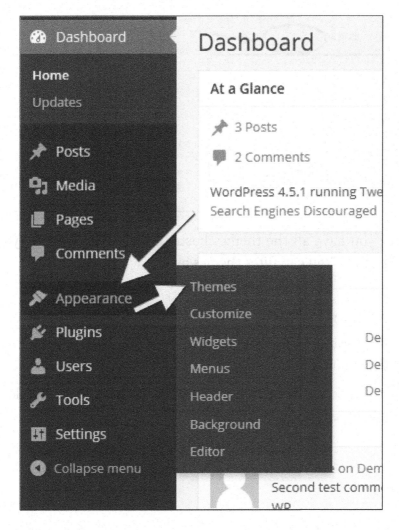

Next, click on the *Add New* button at the top of the *Themes* screen.

Now you have all the themes hosted on WordPress.org at your fingertips. You can filter themes by

- Featured
- Popular
- Latest
- Favourites

Or, if you know the name of the theme you want to download, simply type it in the textbox:

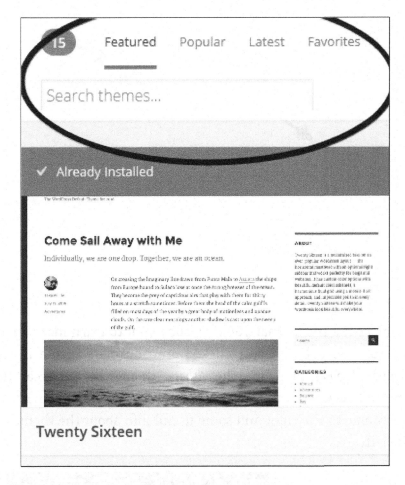

You can also perform more granular searches. Click on the *Feature Filter* button and select the relevant checkboxes in the available filtering criteria:

- Colours
- Layout
- Features
- Subject

Then click on the *Apply Filters* button.

If you spot a theme that you like, click on it to learn more about it. For instance, I've just clicked on a business theme in the *Popular Themes* tab. It's the *Athena* theme, by Smartcat (its Theme Check score is 100%!) . The new screen has a preview of the theme to the right and some useful info about the theme on the left.

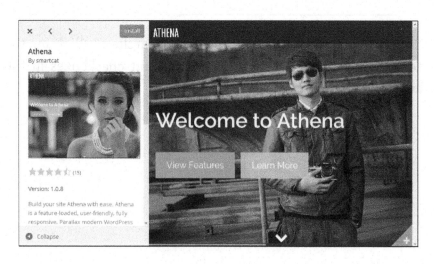

If you're ready to try out your theme, click on the *Install* button and WordPress takes care of the rest.

If everything goes according to plan, you should see a success message and the link to activate the theme. Go ahead and click on *Activate* and check out your website.

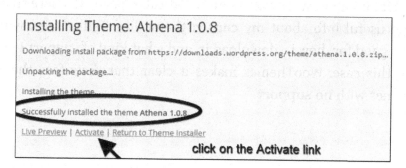

That's it, your theme is now installed!

Installing your theme from a themes marketplace

There are tons of marketplaces to choose from. Here are just a few that I think are great:

- Themeforest
- WooThemes
- Elegant Themes
- iThemes
- StudioPress

Some of these marketplaces have a limited range of free themes. For demonstration purposes, and for the fact that we're not trying to sell you anything. I'll download a free theme from WooThemes, the company originally behind the well known WordPress e-commerce plugin WooCommerce. This is convenient if you're thinking of setting up your online shop, because all themes from Woo have WooCommerce support baked in.

I'm on the WooThemes website on the Free themes page. Let's say, Mystile is the theme I'd like to use for my website. I click on it and now I'm on the theme's dedicated page. It's here that I get useful info about my chosen theme like its features, what it's good for, how to download it, and what kind of support I get. In this case, WooThemes makes it clear that their free theme comes with **no support**.

To download the theme I first need to click the Add to Cart button and go through the checkout process.

Free Theme Package

- Mystile is a free download.
- Our free themes are built on the same WooFramework that our commercial themes are.
- **Support is not included for this theme**, if you would like support please purchase a product from WooThemes to gain access to all our support resources.
- You need to add this theme to your cart and checkout in order to have access to it. This will also assign you a license key to activate 2-click updates via the WooThemes Helper plugin.

If you don't already have a WooThemes account you'll need to create one before proceeding to checkout.

Once the checkout process is successful, I'm presented with a page containing the details of my purchase and links to:

- download my theme
- view my subscription key (which I'm going to copy somewhere safe on my computer)
- read my theme's documentation.

Next, I download my theme's ZIP file to my computer desktop and go to the *Themes* panel of my WordPress dashboard. I click the *Add New* button and then the *Upload Theme* button.

I now browse to the location of my theme's files on my desktop by clicking the *Browse* button and select the ZIP folder with my theme's name.

Finally, I click on *Install Now*, and WordPress takes care of unzipping the archive file and installing the theme. At the end of the process I get the same message WordPress displayed previously when installing the theme from WordPress.org, and I can go ahead and activate my new theme.

The *Themes* screen in the dashboard displays all the themes already installed on your site. From there you can:

- **search** for an installed theme
- select an installed theme to **read the theme's details**
- **preview** an installed theme and even try out its built-in customization options before activation
- **activate** an installed theme.

If you have many WordPress themes installed on your site and you're looking for a specific one, the search feature at the top of the *Themes* panel will save you some time.

As soon as you type the name of the theme you're looking for, WordPress instantly makes it available to you.

To preview an installed theme, just hover your mouse over it and click the *Live Preview* button.

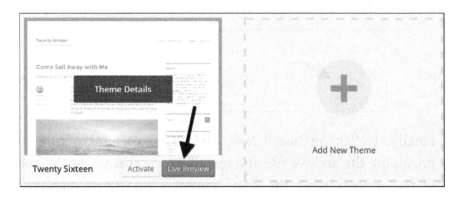

Doing so gives you access to the *Theme Customizer* panel, the amazing built-in customization tool WordPress uses to give you customization power over your theme. A limited number of options are provided by WordPress itself, therefore they're always available, no matter which theme you use. Everything else you find are courtesy of the specific theme you're using. As a consequence, switching themes means losing your customizations.

I'll go into more details about the *WordPress Customizer* later, for now just be aware that you can configure some modification settings listed on the left of the screen and see their effect displayed in real time on the right-hand side of the panel.

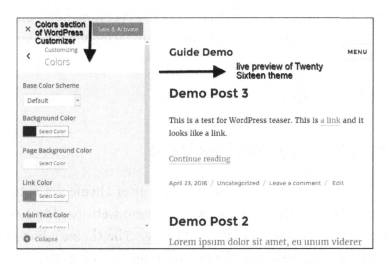

As long as you don't save your changes, you don't need to worry about messing up your theme. Also, because you're experimenting on a theme that's not active, your modifications won't be showing on the live site.

Finally, you can make any installed theme active by clicking on the *Activate* button that appears on mouse hover.

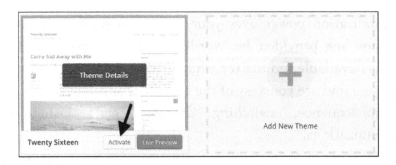

That's all there's to installing and activating a WordPress theme.

To get the most out of your theme, there's still some work to be done. Stuff like adding and configuring recommended plugins, uploading the correctly-sized images, updating your menus and widgets, etc.

Let's find out more.

4.3 Configuring a WordPress Theme

One of the most common complaints after theme activation is that the theme doesn't look like the demo website. Most of the times, however, this is not a bad thing. The theme's live demo is there to showcase the theme and illustrate all of the theme's capabilities. Obviously, almost only very simple themes look like the live demo out of the box.

You'll find that some themes make available some dummy content that you can import into WordPress and have your website instantly resemble the theme's demo site. I don't recommend you take this route mainly because you don't want your website to have the same text and pictures as the theme's demo website. Furthermore, if you'll have your website magically turned into the theme's demo site, you'll have a harder time understanding how to add your own content and images without messing up the theme's structure.

The guideline I'm going to follow here is: **learn the theme's documentation and configure your theme on the basis of the information you find there using your own text and images.** Great documentation is what I consider to be the one most important tool in your DIY toolbox - make sure your theme has it.

Setting up the homepage

If your website is not just a blog, but the public face of your business on the Internet, make sure you choose a theme with a great-looking homepage.

By default, WordPress displays a list of the ten most recent blog posts on the homepage. To change this, you need to perform a simple configuration step.

Create a new page for the homepage

To begin with, create a new page by going to *Pages -> Add New* from the dashboard main menu. Enter *Home* as the page title and click *Publish*.

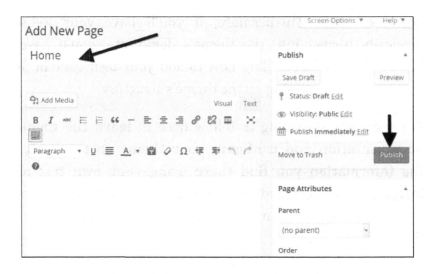

Create a new page for the Blog page

Now create another page by following the same process. Use *Blog* or *News* (or whatever title you want to give your blog page) as your page title.

Adjust the Front Page settings

Finally go to *Settings -> Reading* from the dashboard main menu. At the moment the default setting is to have *Your latest posts* as your website's front page display option. To change that, simply click on the *A static page* radio button.

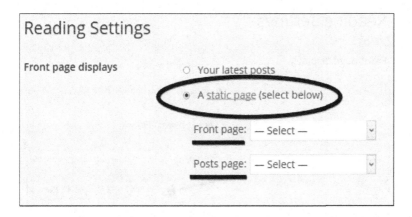

Now you have access to the *Front page* and *Posts page* dropdown boxes. Select *Home* from the *Front page* dropdown box and *Blog* (or whatever you called your blog page) from the *Posts page* dropdown box.

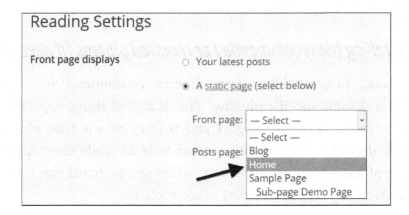

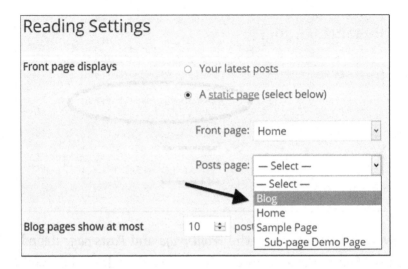

Finally, click on the *Save Changes* button and visit your website's homepage. You should now see a static page and not the list of your latest blog posts.

Installing the recommended or required plugins (if needed)

To add functionality, some themes recommend (or even require) some specific plugins. This is a good thing: separation of concerns between plugins and themes means that plugins look after the functionality of your website while themes take care of its appearance. This way, when you switch themes, your functionality will still be part of your website.

I'll talk more about plugins in the next chapter.

Menus locations

Themes decide where to display your website menu. This means that when you activate a new theme, you'll need to make sure your navigation is still displayed properly. If it isn't, you need to go to *Appearance -> Menus* from the dashboard main navigation and change the *Theme location* in the *Menu Settings* section.

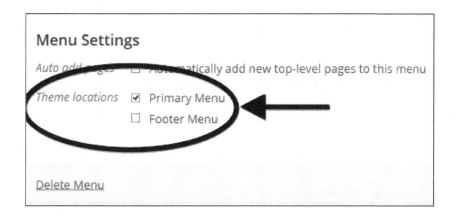

Themes widget areas

Themes also decide where on your website you can display widgets. If you switch themes, it's possible that widgets you placed on the website while using a previous theme don't look quite as good, or don't even get displayed at all in the new theme.

To solve this, you need to access *Appearance -> Widgets* from the dashboard main menu and get familiar with the widgets-ready areas or sidebars in your new theme. If necessary, add your widgets again in the new locations.

For instance, these are the widget-ready areas in the free *Athena* theme:

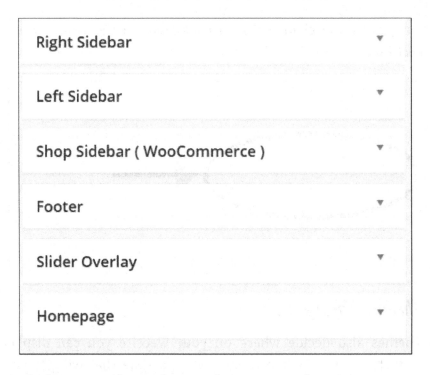

And these are the widget-ready areas in the *Twenty Sixteen* default WordPress theme:

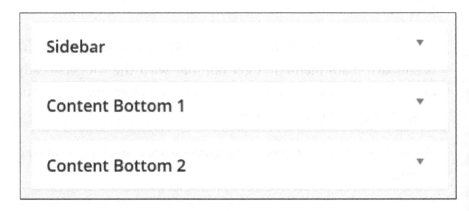

Quite a bit of difference!

Just be aware that, if your widgets look odd or don't display where you expect them to when you switch themes, you need to add your widgets again to the appropriate widget-ready areas your new theme makes available.

Take care of your website's images

A few things spoil a website's professional appearance as much as wrongly sized or poor quality images. If images are too big or too small, they can break your website's layout. Also, the wrong aspect ratio (the ratio between width and height) makes your images look squashed and cheap.

WordPress creates three image sizes each time you upload an image into the Media Library:

● Thumbnail
● Medium
● Full-size

Since version 4.4, WordPress is smart enough to serve the right image size on the basis of the device your website is being viewed on. This is great because visitors on a slow Internet connection will be spared the long wait and possibly high cost that come with image-heavy sites being downloaded through their mobile devices.

It's important, however, that you crop your images to the size that best fits the design of your theme. Because each theme is different, a good theme always informs its users about the recommended size for the main images in its documentation.

For instance, the documentation for the *Twenty Sixteen* theme on WordPress.com has a section where it specifies the correct measurements for its images:

If you stick to those recommendations, your images will look great.

Another gotcha as far as images are concerned, is uploading images straight from your camera into your website. Doing so with just a few images can slow down your site considerably. Slow sites don't attract visitors, are not mobile-friendly, and Google tends to penalize them.

To avoid these undesirable consequences, after cropping your images to the recommended width and height, use an **image compression tool** to compress their file size to an optimum level. Image editors usually come equipped with image compression features. You don't have to use something expensive like Photoshop to take care of your images, a free online image editor like Pixlr will do just fine.

Finally, it's always a good idea to compress your image further using online services like TinyPNG, which is great for both JPG and PNG images.

4.4 Customizing a WordPress Theme

Most WordPress themes ship with handy customization options that you can set without the need to know any coding languages. Themes developed according to WordPress.org standards only use the WordPress Customizer for theme options.

WordPress Customizer

What and how much you can change in your theme using built-in, no-code-required options depends on the theme you're using.

You can access the *Customizer* straight from the WordPress toolbar, which appears on the front-end of your website when you're logged in:

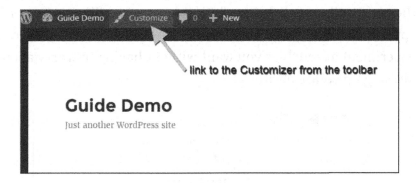

Or you can get to the *Customizer* page from *Appearance -> Customize* in the dashboard main menu:

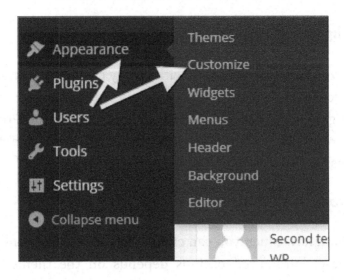

The beauty of the *Customizer* is that you have all your customization options conveniently located in clearly labelled panels and sections on the left of the screen, while your theme is displayed on the right. As you make your modifications, the *Customizer* shows a live preview of what they look like on your theme. Until you click *Save & Publish*, your modifications won't appear on the live site, which is cool because you can experiment as much as you want without having to worry about messing up your website.

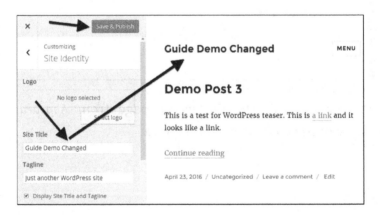

Custom CSS editor

If you know some CSS (Cascading Style Sheet), the language for styling your web pages, you can have much more control over the look and feel of your theme. Stuff like colors, fonts, text size, etc., can all be manipulated using CSS.

The important point is: NEVER EVER CHANGE YOUR THEME'S FILES DIRECTLY.

If you change your theme's files, you'll lose your modifications on the next theme update. To make CSS customizations, use a custom CSS editor instead. Your modified styles will not be part of the theme's files, therefore they'll still be there after you've updated to the next version of your theme.

Some themes come with a custom CSS editor bundled up out of the box. If your theme doesn't have one, you can install a free custom CSS editor plugin like Advanced CSS Editor, Customizer Custom CSS, and Simple Custom CSS, to mention just a few of those available on the WordPress.org plugins repository.

Conclusion

At the end of this chapter you've learned some good tips on how to choose a great WordPress theme for your business, how to install and activate it on your website, and how to make simple customizations using the *WordPress Customizer*.

Congratulations!

Now it's time for you to be introduced to what makes WordPress so awesome to build all kinds of websites under the sun: plugins.

CHAPTER 5:

WordPress Plugins

In this chapter you're going to learn how to install and manage a WordPress plugin on your website. I will also suggest the best WordPress plugins for must-have features like:

- SEO
- security & backup
- contact form
- mailing list
- social sharing

Let's get started!

5.1 What Are Plugins?

WordPress does pretty amazing things out of the box. So far you've created and customized web pages, web menus, and blog posts without touching a line of code.

The strength of WordPress is that you can easily extend its core functionality with a few clicks using plugins.

A plugin is a piece of software that you install on your WordPress website to add specific features, e.g., contact forms, social media integration, ecommerce, etc.

5.2 Managing WordPress Plugins

WordPress plugins, just like themes, can be free, freemium and paid. The most reliable place where you can get free plugins is the WordPress.org plugins repository, where at the time of writing you can freely download and experiment with over 44,400 plugins.

To access the plugins panel in your WordPress dashboard, click on *Plugins->Installed Plugins* from the main menu:

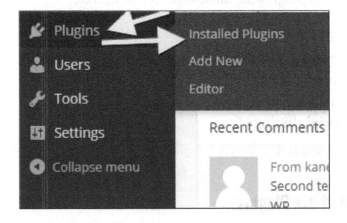

From this panel you can manage all your plugins in a similar way to WordPress themes.

Deleting a WordPress Plugin

By default, WordPress bundles two plugins - *Akismet* and *Hello Dolly*.

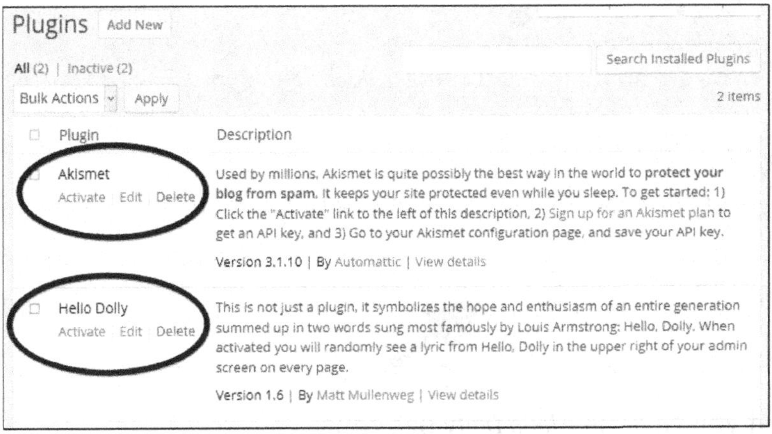

Akismet is a great anti-spam plugin you might want to try on your website if you start to get too many spam comments.

Hello Dolly is just a sample plugin that doesn't really do anything except displaying a random line from Louis Armstrong's song of the same name. This plugin is authored by Matt Mullenweg, WordPress creator, and it has some kind of sentimental link to WordPress history.

For security reasons, it's recommended that you delete all plugins that you don't use on your website. Start by deleting *Hello Dolly*.

Select the checkbox next to *Hello Dolly* and click the *Delete* link:

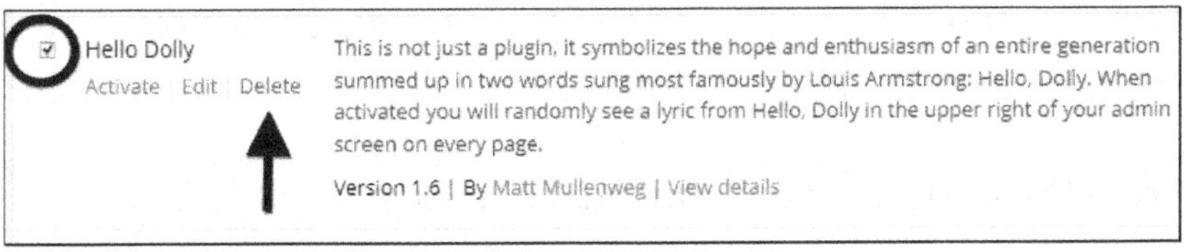

Confirm that you want to delete the plugin:

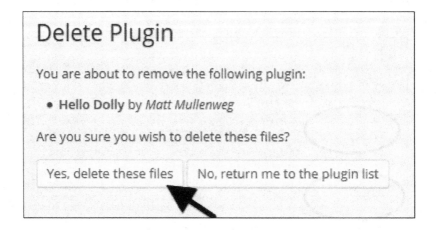

And you're done, *Hello Dolly* has gone:

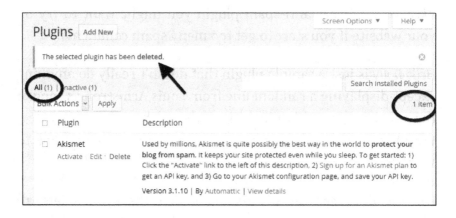

Adding WordPress plugins

Adding a plugin is not different from adding a WordPress theme. If you're looking for a plugin hosted in the WordPress.org plugins repository, you can have access to it straight from the Plugins panel of your WordPress installation.

From the Dashboard main menu, go to *Plugins -> Add New*.

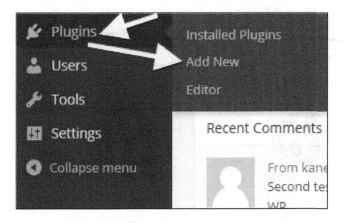

You now have access to the plugins in the repo, which you can filter by:

- Featured
- Popular
- Recommended
- Favorites

If you know the name of the plugin you're looking for, you can type it in the search box.

If you've downloaded a plugin or purchased your plugin from the author's website or a marketplace, you can click on the *Upload Plugin* button at the top of the screen:

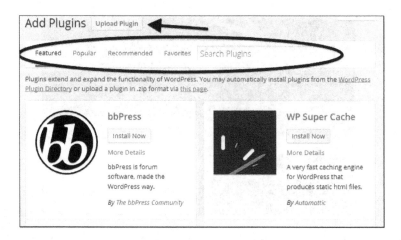

Once the unzipped plugin files are in your WordPress installation, you can see it displayed in the Plugins panel. Just click *Activate* to make the plugin's functionality available to your website:

Some plugins implement their functionality out of the box after activation, others require some data from you before they're ready to do their job.

If your plugin needs some data, e.g., portfolio items if it's a portfolio plugin, products and payment gateway data if it's a shopping cart, etc., simply access the plugin settings panel in your website's back-end and provide the information in the appropriate input boxes. Each plugin is different so each one will have its own requirements and configuration options. In the next chapter, you'll see how to configure the WooCommerce plugin to set up a shopping cart on your website.

The best plugins are well documented, therefore make sure you check out the plugin's documentation page for more details. If you get stuck, look for support either in the WordPress.org forums or the plugin's website - if you paid for your plugin, support is usually included in what you paid for.

That's it, now you can add and remove functionality to your WordPress website at the click of a button!

5.3 Essential Features for Your Website You Can Add with Plugins

There are some pieces of functionality a modern business website can't do without. Below, I've prepared a list of must-have features and some of the best, most supported and reliable WordPress plugins you need to implement them on your website.

Choosing from the tons of plugins available out there can be tough, so I hope this curated selection will be of help as you set up your website.

SEO

Your prospective clients need to find your website quickly on search engines. Some would say that making a website search-engine-ready is a job best left to the professionals. However, with Google changing its algorithm on a regular basis, nobody can make sure your website will always be number 1 on the search results list.

This is not to say that there's nothing to be done. On the contrary, Google offers a wealth of information about what you can do to improve the quality of your website and optimize it for search engine crawlers. The official Google's SEO Starter Guide will get you started on the basics in no time. Following these guidelines will increase your chances of your website getting a good position in organic search results.

WordPress is SEO-friendly out of the box because it:

- uses valid code
- is accessibility-aware
- provides easy to configure meaningful URLs using permalinks
- gives you the option to add meaningful titles and descriptions to posts, pages and images
- offers an easy way to add alternative text for images.

These are all great ways of making sure your website plays nice with search engines.

For those who want to probe further, the industry-standard plugin for SEO is certainly Yoast SEO by Joost de Valk.

With over 1 million active installs, this plugin and its various add-ons give you all you need to optimize your website for search engines. More than that, it guides you towards a focus keyword and makes sure you use that keyword an appropriate number of times in your content.

Website Security & Backup

Because WordPress is super popular, it's an irresistible target for hackers. WordPress core is very secure and in continuous development. Although non developers can get annoyed with fast-paced updates, these are a great way to protect the platform against malicious attacks. However, there's a list of vulnerabilities you should be paying attention to:

- server vulnerabilities
- theme security
- plugin security
- file permissions
- securing specific files (like wp-admin, wp-config and wp-includes)
- database security
- computer vulnerabilities
- FTP vulnerabilities

The plugins listed below can't guarantee that your website will never get hacked, which is impossible, but will significantly decrease the risk.

iThemes Security

As one of the most popular WordPress security plugins, iThemes Security is available both as a free and a premium version.

iThemes is great against most of the common security issues including:

- brute force protection.
- monitoring core files for any changes.
- hiding both the login and admin pages.
- locking out users who enter their username or password incorrectly too many times.
- two-Factor authentication.
- logging user actions.
- forcing secure passwords for specific user roles and file permissions.
- ticketed support is also available to all pro users.

There are a few things you need to be aware of before using iThemes Security. If you're installing the plugin on an existing site, there is a possibility that some of the changes might break your site, especially with regard to the changes the plugin makes to the database and to the path of your wp-content directory. As a precaution, you should backup your website before activating the plugin or enabling any new features.

WordFence

Wordfence is another plugin that follows the popular freemium model. Depending on how many licenses you purchase and how long each license is valid for, Wordfence can offer you some fairly attractive discounts.

Wordfence is great at performing the following tasks:

- scanning for file changes
- blocking IP addresses
- two-factor authentication
- country blocking and country redirects
- custom alerts

Wordfence can be a great asset when it comes to website security and it has fewer risks of causing problems compared to some of the other plugins.

All in One WP Security

All in One WP Security currently shows over 300,000 active installs.

This plugin uses a grading system to make it easier for you to spot the areas where your website's security can be improved.

Using All in One WP Security comes with some risk of breaking your site. To reduce this risk, the plugin implements three categories of changes – **basic, intermediate** and **advanced**. You can safely set the basic features, while the intermediate and advanced configurations increase the likelihood of breaking some of your website's functionality. If you come up against any problems, you'll find useful instructions on how to fix them.

Each primary security feature comes with a detailed description so you know exactly what settings you're configuring.

Among the security features this plugin offers are:

- option to disable the WP Meta information
- monitoring user accounts for vulnerabilities
- brute Force login attack prevention
- manual user registration approval
- ability to change the database tables' prefix

- protection of specific files
- blacklisting users based upon their IP address or a range of IP addresses
- basic firewall protection
- changing the login page URL, cookie based logins as well as Captchas and whitelists
- comment spam prevention
- detection of changes in files
- preventing users from copying your website's text.

Sucuri Security

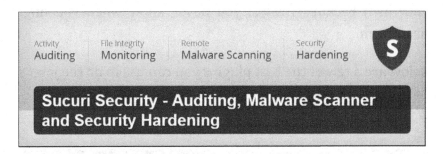

You can download Sucuri Security for free from the WordPress.org repository.

The plugin is mainly designed to alert you to potential problems with your website.

Sucuri can help you with the following four areas:

- monitoring and recording of all activity on your website
- monitoring of all files such as WordPress core files, themes and plugins
- Sucuri's free scanner monitors your website for malware

● Hardening of your website's security, e.g., removing the WordPress version information, restricting access to some directories like wp-content and wp-includes, etc.

Having a clean and updated backup is the best way you can prepare for the worst. In the unfortunate circumstance of your website being hacked or your server getting wiped out, you'll be able to restore your website without any loss in no time.

Some hosting companies offer website backups as a service, either at an additional fee or included with your hosting fee. However, it's better to err on the side of caution and also have your own backups ready... you never know when you might need them.

Below are a few of the best plugins you can use to do the job.

VaultPress

Matt Mullenweg (WordPress co-founder) and his team at Automattic are behind VaultPress.

VaultPress is a subscription based service with different plans and pricing offering automated, real-time cloud backups.

Setting up VaultPress and restoring your website from backups is just a matter of clicks. Some of their packages also include security scans.

BackupBuddy

Among the most popular paid backup plugins is BackupBuddy by iThemes. This plugin lets you easily schedule your own backups on a daily, weekly or monthly schedule. You can conveniently store your backups on Dropbox, Amazon S3, Rackspace Cloud, Stash (iThemes cloud service), or have them emailed to your inbox.

BackupBuddy is not subscription-based. You have four pricing plans available to you, which allow you to use the plugin on a set number of websites and give you access for a year to premium support forums, regular updates, and 1GB of storage space on Stash.

UpdraftPlus

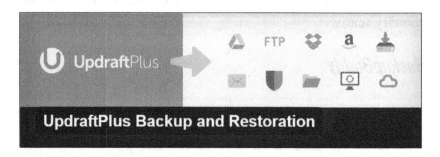

UpdraftPlus allows you to create a complete backup of your WordPress site, store it on the cloud or download it to your computer.

The plugin lets you create scheduled backups, which you can then store in your chosen location. A premium version of UpdraftPlus offers additional features and addons.

Caching

Your business website must load fast into your clients' browsers, every second's delay is likely to lead to fewer potential customers, which will eventually hurt your bottom line.

Google has also started to penalize websites that take too long to load, and getting to the wrong side of Google is certainly something you'll want to avoid.

If you're just creating your very first website, you won't have much content yet, therefore it's unlikely your website has serious performance problems. However, it's important that you plan for the future. Once your content grows and performance starts to become an issue, you'll be ahead of the game.

Caching is one of the best tools for speeding up your website. If a web page hasn't changed, there's no need for the browser to send a request for all the assets needed by that page, e.g., images, videos, HTML, CSS stylesheets, etc. and for the server to gather those resources and send them back to the browser, each time that page is loaded. With caching in place, the browser caches that page, so when users access it, the browser has a copy ready for display without having to make a new server request.

You can easily add caching functionality to your WordPress website using plugins that work by creating a static version of your content and displaying it on the browser. You'll be able to see a significant improvement in website performance in no time, and your visitors will have a much better experience.

Check out these caching plugins - they're all very popular and some of them are freely available from the WordPress.org plugins repository.

W3 Total Cache

At the time of writing, W3 Total Cache boasts more than one million active WordPress installs.

The plugin has tons of features, which is great for flexibility. However, this also means that some users can feel a bit overwhelmed by the choices. The good news is that the default settings should work on most WordPress websites, so you can simply activate it and W3 Total Cache does its job.

Caching features include page cache, database cache, browser cache, CDN, and monitoring. You also have a debug option and import and export functionality.

WP Super Cache

WP Super Cache is another super popular plugin on the WordPress.org plugins repository.

You find seven tabs in the options page displaying easy-to-configure settings. Just enable caching on the *Easy* tab and WP Super Cache will start caching your pages. The *Contents* tab will contain information on how many pages the plugin has cached and how many pages have expired.

This is a feature-rich but user-friendly plugin.

WP Rocket

WP Rocket is a premium plugin — in order to use it on your website, you need to purchase a license.

Although the free alternatives listed above are great, you could consider WP Rocket as an investment rather than a cost for your business.

To begin with, a benchmarking test performed by marketing expert Philip Blomsterberg points to WP Rocket as the fastest choice available on the market.

Although the plugin has advanced options to fine-tune your caching operations, it offers a user-friendly and well-designed interface that affords great results with minimal effort on the user's part.

You can also count on fantastic tech support ready to help out in case you're stuck.

Contact Form

Contact forms are an essential feature of any business website. Your clients need to know how to get in touch with you, and displaying a well-designed, easy to access form is the best way to make sure you don't miss any opportunities.

WordPress doesn't offer contact forms out of the box. But fear not, there are well over 1600 contact form plugins out there to choose from.

Here are three fantastic contact form plugins for WordPress you can consider for your website.

Gravity Forms

Gravity Forms is the Swiss army knife of WordPress developers. There's little you can't accomplish with this plugin, but it's not available for free. Besides the obvious contact form, with the help of add-ons you can create all kinds of engaging content like surveys and quizzes.

In case you get stuck, Gravity Forms makes available FAQs, knowledge base, forums, and email support, so you might want to think about investing in such a versatile and well supported product as this.

Ninja Forms

Ninja Forms is freely downloadable from the WordPress.org plugins repository. This plugin lets you create highly interactive forms without much hassle.

You can do a lot more with Ninja Forms if you purchase its premium extensions. For instance, you can connect the plugin to Campaign Monitor, Freshbooks, SMS notifications, etc.

If you need help at any point, you can turn to the Ninja Forms community support forum, the plugin's documentation and email support.

Contact Form 7

Contact Form 7 is still the most popular free contact form plugin hosted on WordPress.org.

The plugin adds a *Contact* section to your WordPress dashboard where you can create new forms and edit existing ones.

Contact Form 7 offers an HTML-based interface, which for users not very familiar with HTML markup can present a few problems. On the other hand, if you dab in code a bit, this feature gives you considerable control over the appearance of your forms.

Once you're done adjusting your form, just grab the shortcode and include it within your post or page.

Mailing List

The most important tool to build your customer base on your business website is an email list.

How many times did you land on a website to be presented with a big bright button asking for your email address, often in exchange for a valuable freebie? Well, that's the most successful way you can get visitors to subscribe to your website and turn them into potential customers for your business. Once you have their email address, it's easy to build relationships with them, find out what they're looking for, what their pain points are, get their opinion on a product or service you're working on, offer special discounts, etc.

Although it happens that people miss status updates on their social media timelines, it's highly unlikely they miss an email in their inbox.

The plugins I'm going to list below make it quick and painless to add list building capabilities to your WordPress website. Check them out.

OptinMonster

<u>OptinMonster</u> is a premium WordPress plugin that lets you add a subscription form inside a popup box. Whatever one might think about them, It looks like popup forms have a very high conversion rate, so you might want to give them a try.

A great feature this plugin has to offer is exit-intent technology. This means that the plugin tracks visitors' mouse movements, and only shows them the pop up at the exact time they're about to leave your website.

One more cool thing you can do with OptinMonster is A/B testing. This kind of testing gives you the chance to add your form to different pages or categories and then monitor the results to verify what works best in terms of conversion rates.

Qualaroo

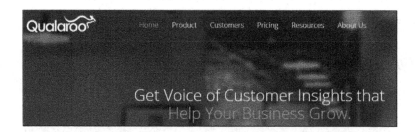

Qualaroo is a paid subscription-based plugin that adds a slide-in form for email subscriptions. Although slide-ins feel less intrusive than popups, conversion rates are higher using popups.

SumoMe

SumoMe is a free plugin with marketing superpowers that you can freely download from WordPress.org.

Among the cool features of this plugin you find:

popup email subscription form

A/B testing for the popup

optional exit-intent technology like OptinMonster

easy integration with major email providers

easy customization

SumoMe also offers social sharing and website analytics. In short, you get the whole package with one free plugin.

Social Sharing

When your readers find something interesting on your website, having buttons for easy sharing functionality increases engagement and therefore drives traffic to your content. More traffic can lead to more conversions, which is good for your business.

Here's a short list of the best social sharing plugins for your business WordPress website.

Monarch

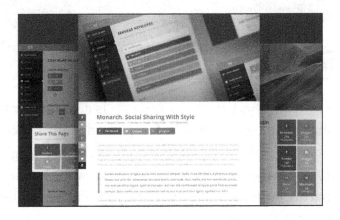

Monarch is a cool premium social sharing WordPress plugin by Elegant Themes.

The location of your social sharing buttons on the page makes quite a bit of difference to the results of your social media promotion. Monarch offers a fair number of placement options so that you can experiment where your social sharing buttons are most effective on your website.

With Monarch you also have an image sharing option. Visuals are great for grabbing people's attention and creating engagement, which is great for the success of your content on social media sites.

Easy Social Share Buttons for WordPress

Easy Social Share Buttons for WordPress is a powerful premium social sharing plugin available for purchase on CodeCanyon. There's hardly anything you can't do with this plugin. For instance, you have options for where you want to place your social sharing buttons, what you want your buttons to look like, post views counter, etc.

SumoMe

As a free social sharing plugin alternative for your WordPress website SumoMe is not only great for adding list building functionality, as I showed you in the previous section, but also social sharing features to your website.

Give it a try!

Conclusion

At the end of this chapter you've learned:

- How to extend WordPress with plugins
- How to install and activate a WordPress plugin
- The best plugins for must-have features for your business website.

Next, you're going to get close and personal with the most popular WordPress ecommerce plugin: **WooCommerce**.

CHAPTER 6:

WooCommerce

If you're eager to find more ways of increasing your bottom line, one of the best options available to you is establishing a strong online presence and selling your products or services on your website.

Thanks to WordPress and WooCommerce, the most popular ecommerce plugin for WordPress, setting up and having full control over your own online shop is something you can do yourself.

In this chapter, I'll show you the basics of using WooCommerce. Although showing you the ins and outs of ecommerce development is well beyond the scope of this chapter, what you find here will give you the confidence to add a simple shop section to your WordPress website and sell your awesome products or services.

In particular, you're going to find out about:

- The benefits of using WooCommerce
- How to Install WooCommerce
- WooCommerce-compatible Themes
- Managing Categories and Products
- WooCommerce shop management tools

6.1 Why Use WooCommerce for Your Online Shop?

If you're reading this guide, chances are you're an awesome entrepreneur, but you're no web designer or developer. Also, you're at the initial stages of your business, when budget is tight and hiring a team of programmers to create a custom ecommerce solution is not a reasonable option.

At this point, concerns you might be having include any of the following:

- **Security** — this is the most sensitive area of concern for an online shop. Things like hacking attacks and server downtime jeopardize your customers' credentials and disrupt the shopping experience. All this amounts to decrease in trust with damaging consequences for your small business
- **Easy customization** — having an online shop that has the cookie-cutter look & feel of hundreds of online shops is not going to help you establish a brand. You need an easy way to tweak and customize your online shop's pages easily, without messing with code
- **User experience** — this has been an increasingly important area of online shopping. The journey from browsing your products to the shopping cart checkout

process needs to be intuitive, engaging and smooth, whatever the device customers use to access your website. This will have a big positive impact on your sales. You might be wondering: but I'm no expert on user experience, and certainly haven't got the budget to hire one.

● **Keeping track of your online shop's performance** — this concern relates to the point I mentioned above. If you notice a drop in sales, you need a way to keep track of your customers' actions on your online shop. This is so because you'll want to know where your customers experience issues with your website. For instance, if a significant number of visitors leave your website just seconds after they've landed on your homepage, it could be they find problems navigating your website or finding what they're looking for. If shopping cart abandonment is the issue, you can improve the checkout process for your customers. To be able to tackle these problems, you'll need some kind of analytical tool that records your website's data, especially your customers' activities, and reports them in a meaningful, easy-to-grasp format. Not being a developer yourself, having to integrate such a tracking system could be keeping you awake at night.

Since its first launch in 2011 by WooThemes, WooCommerce was an instant success: free, open source, and super user-friendly. In 2013 this ecommerce plugin went through a complete makeover, which resulted in WooCommerce 2.0. To boost its credibility even further, in May 2015 Automattic, the company behind WordPress itself, bought WooCommerce. The plugin powers millions of online stores, it's easy to get started with, and has a low learning curve, at least if you don't require extensive customizations of its default functionality.

Benefits of Using WooCommerce

If you want to sell some products or services from your self-hosted WordPress website, here are just some of the things that make WooCommerce a great option for you:

● **User-friendliness** — WooCommerce lets you do lots of stuff out of the box, no need to know PHP or any other coding language. You can categorize your products by price, variations such as size, color, and more; you can sell products (physical, downloadable and affiliate products) and services (which WooCommerce calls *virtual products*).

The interface WooCommerce creates in your WordPress back-end is very intuitive: you can easily configure options that make WooCommerce one of the most flexible plugins on offer today.

You can monitor your customers' actions so that you know exactly which products get the most interest, how many visitors to your website convert into customers, and which orders they've made. Customers can track their orders and receive status updates on the delivery of their goods. With WooCommerce you can also set shipping options and taxes. You have all these goodies available in a single free, open source plugin!

● **Easy customization** — there are tons of themes optimized to work with WooCommerce. But even in the event your theme isn't, the plugin's great code structure and documentation make it easy to customize the display of your shop's pages. Also, there are many add-ons that will let you customize the appearance of your online shop even further without touching a single line of code.

- **Easy integration with any existing WordPress website** — WooCommerce's code base follows best WordPress coding practices, therefore it integrates seamlessly with any WordPress website without any additional work.

- **Security** — WordPress is kept secure by thousands of developers all over the globe. Any security hole gets patched up quickly and updates are available to all installations right away. WooCommerce follows the same pattern of regular updates, compatibility tests with the latest version of WordPress, and frequent security patches.

- **Extensibility** — there's a crowded ecosystem of WooCommerce extensions, both free and paid, which makes it a breeze to add new functionality to your online store. Integrating a new payment gateway or a newsletter subscription service to your online store has never been easier.

- **Getting help** — what if you get stuck? This is one major concern you, as an entrepreneurs setting up an online shop, could be entertaining right now. WooCommerce has you covered with a number of options. You can visit the WooThemes' support page, where you'll find access to a forum, knowledge base, documentation, videos, and ticket-based support. Keep in mind that there's a number of services and freelancers specializing in offering WooCommerce support — they're just a Google search away from you.

Time to get started!

6.2 Installing WooCommerce

You install WooCommerce like any other WordPress plugin. Just go to *Plugins* -> *Add New* from the main menu in your WordPress dashboard.

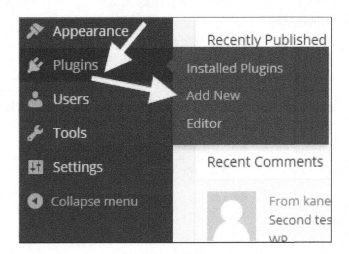

On the *Add Plugins* panel, type woocommerce in the search box at the top:

Next, press *Enter*. WooCommerce should be the first choice in the search results panel:

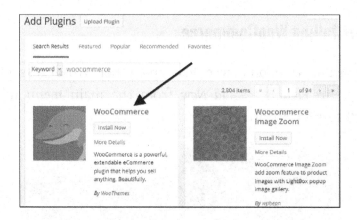

Click on *Install Now* and let WordPress do its job. When the plugin is installed, activate it:

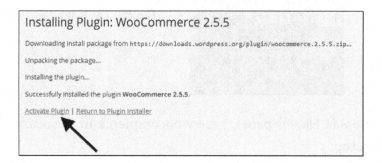

As soon as you do that, WooCommerce displays a quick setup wizard that takes you through the basic steps. This is totally optional, but it's the easiest road to getting started quickly for someone who's completely new to WooCommerce. Furthermore, you can still modify and fine-tune your settings' configurations at any time.

Click on *Let's Go* to get started:

Page Setup

Your WooCommerce shop needs the following pages to work properly:

- Shop
- Cart
- Checkout
- My Account

As the first step in the setup wizard, WooCommerce lets you create these pages at the click of a button.

To do so, go ahead and click *Continue*:

Store Locale

The next step in the setup wizard lets you adjust localization settings for your shop, like shop's location, currency, etc.

Make your adjustments according to your location and click the *Continue* button.

Shipping & Tax

Next, you'll configure a couple of basic settings regarding shipping and taxes. If you plan on selling physical goods, select the appropriate checkbox. This will give you access to more settings you need to specify, i.e., domestic and international shipping costs.

If you're going to charge sales tax, select the appropriate checkbox and fill out the rest of the form with the necessary information.

When you're done, click the *Continue* button:

Payments

Out of the box, WooCommerce lets you configure PayPal Standard as your online payment method. The default offline payment methods are:

- Cheque
- Cash on delivery
- Bank transfer (BACS)

To enable PayPal Standard, just enter your PayPal email address in the designated textbox.

For additional options, you'll need to grab the corresponding WooCommerce extensions, e.g., Stripe Payment Gateway WooCommerce Addon to add Stripe support to your WooCommerce shop, Authorize.net Payment Gateway for WooCommerce to add Authorize.net integration with your WooCommerce shop, etc.

As a side note, keep in mind that, while PayPal Standard takes customers to the PayPal website for payment processing, all the other payment gateways work on your own website. This means that your website must use **SSL** (Secure Sockets Layer) to encrypt all the information between your customers' browsers and the web server. Websites using SSL show that reassuring green padlock in the browser's address bar and use *https* instead of *http*:

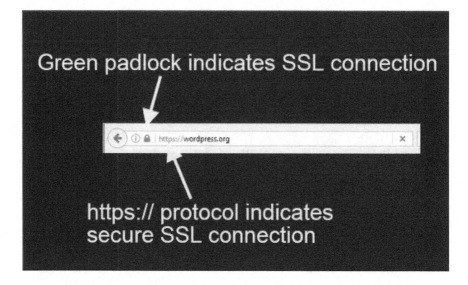

My advice is to go for SSL even if you're using PayPal Standard as a payment method. Here's a couple of reasons:

- Ecommerce websites need to inspire complete trust in their customers. Customers need to feel their account information is secure at all times. If the information between browser and server is not encrypted, users' data can be easily sniffed by anyone on the internet, thereby putting your online customers' data at risk. In short, an ecommerce website without the green padlock doesn't send the right message
- Google considers SSL a ranking factor. Websites using SSL, be they ecommerce sites or any other kind of website, will score more points on Google's algorithm, which means higher chances to be on top of search results. As a business owner, you know how important your placement on the search results is for conversions and sales.

To have SSL on your website, the easiest way is to ask your hosting provider for guidance. Most providers sell and install

SSL certificates, which makes the entire procedure quite painless. Better to think about SSL when you're just getting started rather than later down the road. In fact, converting an existing website to SSL is usually a bit of a hassle, and it's better left in the hands of an expert.

Back to WooCommerce setup wizard: make your selection of payment methods and click *Continue*:

Now your WooCommerce shop is ready!

These are just the fundamental settings you need to get started. For a detailed tutorial on WooCommerce settings, a visit to the WooCommerce 101 video series on Settings is well worth your time.

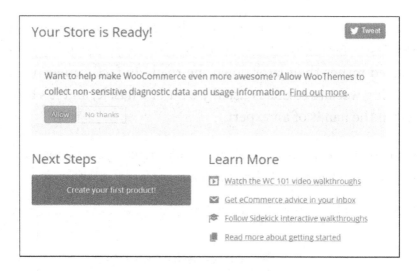

To return to your WordPress dashboard, click on the appropriate link at the bottom of the wizard's page:

Before adding your products, let's dive into the topic of themes. As you're going to see shortly, for the correct display of your WooCommerce-generated pages, it's crucial to put some thought into your choice of theme.

6.3 Is Your WordPress Theme WooCommerce-compatible?

As you know, themes control the look and feel of your website, including the page layout. If you let WooCommerce create the Shop page and other key pages, which you did if you followed along with the basic WooCommerce setup, it's possible that the HTML structure and the CSS styles used in your theme and those used by WooCommerce templates don't match up. When this happens, the result can be a broken layout on the default WooCommerce pages, e.g., Shop, Cart, etc.

If you notice anything like this going on in your website right now, it's highly likely that your theme doesn't offer WooCommerce support.

To have confirmation of this, check your WordPress Admin panel: is it displaying this message?

If so, there's no doubt about it: your theme needs to be made WooCommerce-compatible. Alternatively, you'll have to select another theme which is WooCommerce-compatible out of the box.

In the demo for this guide I'm going to use a free WooCommerce-compatible theme by WooThemes — Mystile.

There are other great themes, both free and paid, which offer WooCommerce support by default. The latest, most popular one by WooThemes is Storefront, freely downloadable from the WordPress.org themes repository. Just do a search and select a WooCommerce-compatible theme that most suits your business goals and taste.

If you absolutely love the theme you're using on your website, but it doesn't offer WooCommerce support by default, then you'll need to fiddle with a little bit of PHP code. This is beyond the scope of this tutorial, but you'll find all the info you need on the WooThemes docs for WooCommerce.

Now that you have your WooCommerce-compatible theme installed and active, it's time to start building a products catalog.

6.4 Managing Categories and Products

Your products make up the most important part of your online shop. Without a product that people want, even the best looking and fully functional online shop hasn't got much chance of success.

WooCommerce allows you to sell physical products, services and downloadable products. You can also sell affiliate products from third-party websites.

Once you know exactly what you're going to sell, who your ideal customers are, and how to reach them, you're ready to start building your WooCommerce catalog.

Product Images

A preliminary step to building your catalog of products, consists in preparing your product images. Images are a key component of an online shop, more important than shop windows are for bricks and mortar shops on the High Street. In fact, you're not present with your potential customers to show them your products in the best possible light. Your products images need to do most of the work for you: they need to look professional and really showcase what you have to offer.

Don't make the **mistake of using high resolution images straight from your digital camera.** Doing so will have a negative impact on page load speed, which is a nightmare for people visiting your website.

Another mistake is to have **wrongly sized images,** either too small or with the wrong aspect ratio. If the image is too small, it could appear pixelated on some high resolution screens. If the image's height and width have the wrong aspect ratio, the image will appear squashed or too elongated. You will want to avoid these outcomes because they will make your shop look unappealing and unprofessional.

Also, it's best to think about this aspect of building your products catalog before adding your very first image. This is so because WooCommerce crops product images to some predefined sizes as soon as you upload them into your WordPress dashboard. You can modify these predefined sizes from your WordPress dashboard, as I'm going to show you shortly. However, if you try to modify the size of images after they're already in your Media Library, you won't be able to do so without using the Regenerate Thumbnails plugin. This is not hard to do, but getting things right from the start is a better option.

For great-looking and fast-loading images follow the two steps below.

#1 Use the right-sized images

You can easily find out what size WooCommerce is going to crop your images to by going to *WooCommerce -> Settings* from the WordPress dashboard main menu:

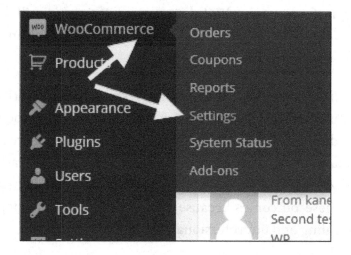

From the *Settings* panel, select the *Products* tab, then the *Display* submenu link:

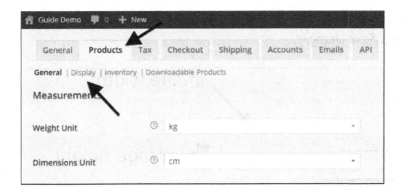

Once you're on the *Display* screen, scroll down until you find the *Product Images* section.

Each time you upload a product image to the Media Library, it crops it to three image sizes:

- **Catalog Images** — cropped to 300 x 300px. You'll find these images displayed on the main Shop page
- **Single Product Image** — cropped to 600 x 600px. These images are displayed in the Single Product page, where WooCommerce showcases a single product in detail
- **Product Thumbnails** — 180 x 180px. These are small images of your products that you can use, for example, in the sidebar or in your website's footer area.

WooCommerce uses a 1:1 aspect ratio, that is, all images are perfect squares.

You can modify both image sizes and aspect ratio, but if you decide to keep them as they are, your graphics have to be perfect squares.

To change these settings, simply enter your desired measurement for the image width on the first textbox and the measurement for the image height on the second textbox and click *Save changes.*

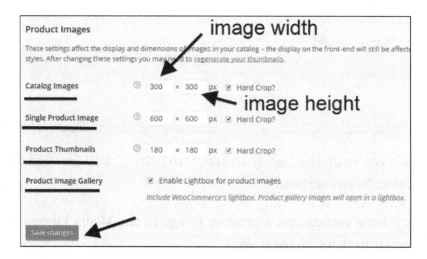

You can choose to upload a big image with the desired aspect ratio for each product and let WooCommerce crop it and create the smaller versions. Alternatively, you can upload images of the biggest size in the image settings, which by default is 600 x 600px, and let WooCommerce create the smaller images for you.

#2 Optimize your images before uploading them to the WordPress Media Library

Let's assume your product images are all 600 x 600px (or the size you defined in the WooCommerce *Image Settings* panel). Before uploading any of the images into the Media Library, make sure you've squeezed every unneeded byte out of them without losing quality. You can do so using your image editing software of choice when you're about to save or export your image to your computer.

Experiment with the image compression levels to decide a good balance between file size and image quality: the lower the image file size the lower the image quality. .JPEG images can usually be optimized to about 80% of their file size without losing quality.

To optimize your images further, use an online image optimizer. You'll find a lot of free options online like TinyPNG , Optimizilla (both good for .PNG and .JPEG image file types), and more.

With your product images ready, it's time to add your first WooCommerce product.

Adding Products

How you want to organize your shop's products is up to you. For example, if you sell various kinds of products, organizing them by categories can be a good idea. If you're only selling a handful of products, categories are a bit of an overkill.

Whatever you decide, keep the focus on your customers: how will your customers find what they're looking for on your shop?

Here's how you add categories to your WooCommerce shop.

How to create a WooCommerce category

Let's say you'd like to sell an awesome collection of teddy bears on your website.

For demo purposes, create the *Teddy Bears* category. All teddy bear products will go into this category. This will make it very easy to browse your shop and keep it manageable.

Go to *Products -> Categories* to access the *Categories* panel from the Dashboard main menu:

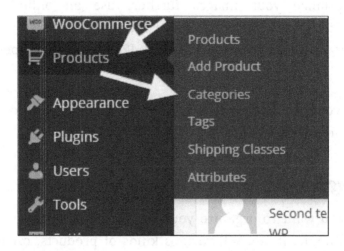

In the *Categories* panel, type the **category name**, **slug** (the lowercase category name for the URL to the category page on your website), **category description**, and add a **category image** (I recommend you upload a 600 x 600px image file — or whatever dimensions you specified for your *Single Product Image* in the *Product Image* settings panel). When you're done, click on *Add New Product Category:*

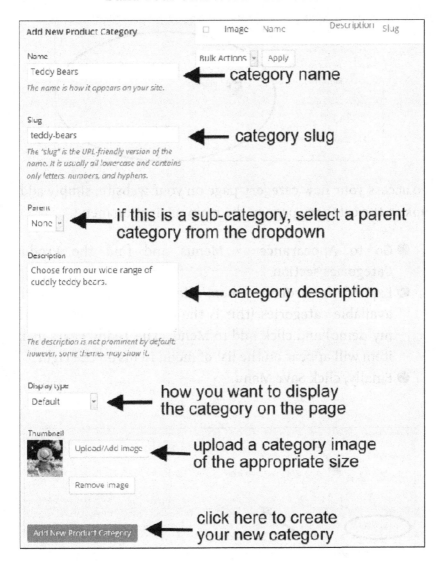

You can edit your categories on the right-hand side of the same panel:

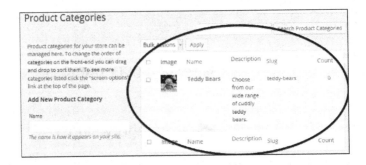

To access your new category page on your website, simply add a link to the category page in the main navigation menu.

- Go to Appearance -> Menus and find the Product Categories section
- Expand the dropdown box, select Teddy Bears from the available categories (this is the only product category in my demo) and click Add to Menu. The Teddy Bears menu item will appear on the list of menu items on the right.
- Finally, click Save Menu.

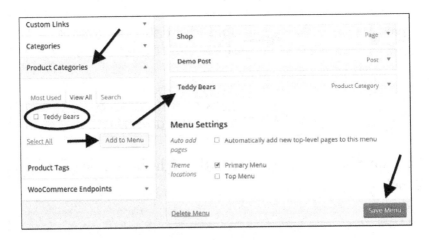

If you now go to the front-end of your website, you'll find a *Teddy Bears* navigation link. Click the link and you'll be on the

Teddy Bears category page. This is what it looks like on my demo:

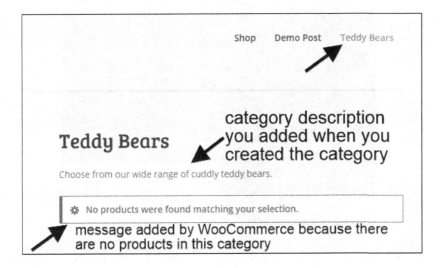

The Mystile theme doesn't display the category image in the category page, it only displays the products belonging to the specified category. To see the category image on the page, you need to display product categories on the Shop page. To do so, your category must contain at least one product.

Go ahead and add a simple teddy bear product to the *Teddy Bears* category.

How to create a simple WooCommerce product

Go to *Products -> Add Product* to access the *Add New Product* editor from the Dashboard main menu:

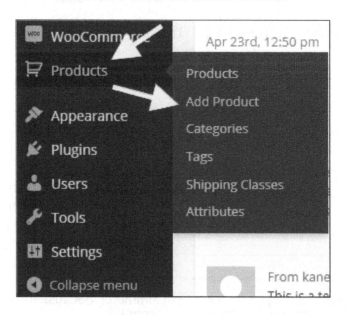

You're going to create a **Simple Product**. In WooCommerce language, a Simple Product is a unique item with no options, which requires shipping.

Once on the *Add New Product* editor, you'll notice that adding a new product is not that much different from adding a blog post:

- Add a Product Name
- Add a Product Description in the text editor
- Add a Product Short Description — this is optional. Think of this as the product version of the post excerpt
- Assign the product to a category — in the demo for this chapter I use the *Teddy Bears* category
- Add product tags
- Add a product image — the image size for this demo is 600 x 600px. This isn't different from the featured image that you can add to regular WordPress posts. If you want to add a gallery showcasing your product in different ways,

click the *Add product gallery images* link and select your images (make sure they're all of the appropriate size).

Before clicking the *Publish* button to create your product there are a few more settings you need to consider in the *Product Data* metabox.

Product Data Metabox

In the *Add New Product* screen you'll find the *Product Data* metabox, where you'll add some important data about your product.

On the left of the metabox there's a vertical menu of links. Clicking a link reveals a number of form controls to gather specific details about your product:

- **General** — in this section, you can add a *SKU* (Stock Keep Unit), which is a number to keep track of your stock. If you use SKU for stock management, add the SKU corresponding to the product you're creating. In this section you can also add a *price* and a *discounted price* if your product is on sale.
- **Inventory** — This section is for managing stock for the individual product. If you disable stock management from the settings page, only the *Manage stock?* option is visible by default.
- **Shipping** — If you're selling a physical product, you'll need to send it over to your customers after purchase. In this section, you can specify things like *product's weight* and *dimensions*, which are important details to determine the correct amount your customers will need to pay in order to cover shipping costs.
- **Linked Products** — *Related products* or *cross-sells* are other products similar or complementary to the product your customer is buying. *Up-sells* are upgrades of the product your customers are buying. You can choose cross-sells and up-sells in this section of the Product Data metabox
- **Attributes** — In this section you can assign attributes to your product. These are technical details you can add to a

product. You can find more on WooCommerce attributes on this documentation page.

● **Advanced** — In this section you can choose to send a *thank you message* to customers after they buy your product. You can also *enable or disable customers' reviews* relative to the individual product you're creating.

Some links in the *Product Data* metabox menu are added or removed according to the type of product you're creating. For instance, if you select the *virtual product* checkbox, the shipping link in the menu will be removed. This is so because virtual products, which are intangible products like services, don't get shipped to your customers as it's the case with physical products. This is great for keeping the form clean and uncluttered.

Feel free to experiment with all the options available. However, in this demo you're going to keep things simple: just add a price for your product in the *Regular Price* textbox

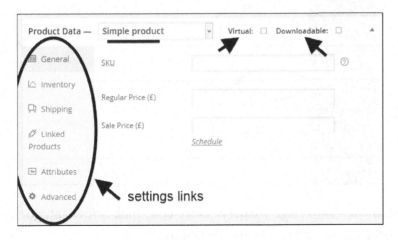

Next, hit the *Publish* button and visit your Shop page. This is what my demo looks like using the Mystile theme:

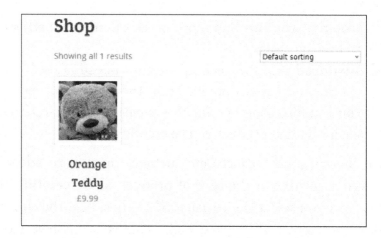

You can also choose to show product categories rather than cluttering your Shop page with all sorts of disparate products.

To do so, go to *WooCommerce -> Settings* and from the *Settings* screen click on the *Products* tab, then on the *Display* submenu link:

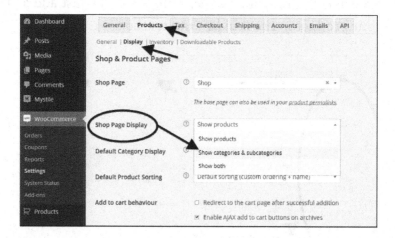

From the Shop Page Display select box, pick Show categories & subcategories and click on Save changes.

Now visit your Shop page again and you should see the *Teddy Bears* category with its featured image:

Clicking on either the category name or image, will land you on a page displaying all products belonging to that category:

Teddy Bears

Choose from our wide range of cuddly teddy bears.

Showing all 1 results   Default sorting ▾

Orange Teddy
£9.99

That's all there is to adding a simple product to your WooCommerce shop. To learn what WooCommerce has to offer regarding all the kinds of product and product-related options at your disposal, head over to the WooCommerce docs on Adding and Managing Products.

6.5 Managing Your WooCommerce Shop

With WooCommerce you not only get to easily add products and integrate a number of payment methods. You can also take advantage of some great tools to manage your online shop.

Coupons

Coupons are a fantastic marketing tool. When used well, they're great for boosting your sales and rewarding your customers.

WooCommerce makes it easy to add coupon codes functionality to your online shop. Let's see how.

Check if coupons are enabled

Before creating a coupon, you need to make sure you have coupons functionality enabled on your website. To do so, go to *WooCommerce -> Settings* from the main Dashboard menu and click on the *Checkout* tab. Make sure the *Enable the use of coupons* checkbox is selected:

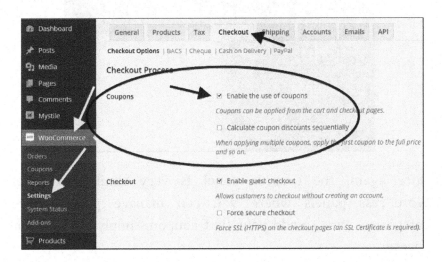

If coupons aren't enabled, select the checkbox and click the *Save changes* button. If they are enabled, you're ready to add your first coupon.

How to add a coupon to your WooCommerce shop

Go to *WooCommerce -> Coupons* from the Dashboard main menu:

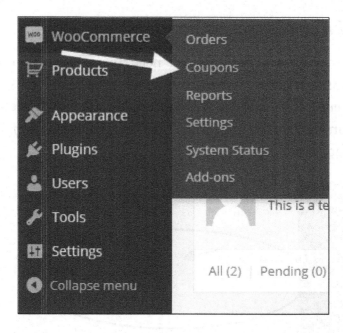

Once again, the *Coupons* panel is very similar to other WordPress panels where you can manage posts, pages, categories, etc. To add your first coupon, simply click on *Add Coupon*:

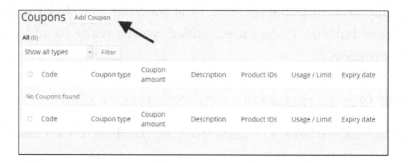

The interface should look familiar to you by now. At the top you add your coupon code and an optional description:

The *Coupon Data* metabox is similar in structure to the *Product Data* metabox you encountered earlier. Clicking a link from the vertical menu on the left reveals a panel with a form to fill out with relevant information regarding your coupon.

The settings to configure in the *General* panel are:

- **Discount type** — you can choose from a *Cart Discount* (a set amount will be discounted from the customer's cart total); *Cart % Discount* (a percentage will be deducted from the customer's cart total); *Product Discount* (a set amount will be discounted from a selected product's price); *Product % Discount* (a percentage will be discounted from a selected product's price).
- **Coupon amount** — this is the value of the coupon. Here you set the discount you're offering either as a set amount or as a percentage on the basis of the discount type you set above.

● **Allow free shipping** — you select this checkbox if you intend to ship items to which the coupon is applied free of charge.

● **Coupon expiry date** — here you can specify the duration of your offer.

In the *Usage Restrictions* panel, you can specify a minimum and a maximum amount your customers need to spend to be able to apply the coupon. Here you can also decide which products or categories you want to include or exclude from the coupon offer:

In the *Usage Limits* panel, you can choose the usage limit per coupon (how many times your customers can use this coupon) and usage limit per user (how many times an individual customer can use this coupon):

For more details on adding coupons with WooCommerce, be sure to visit the WooCommerce docs on Coupon Management.

WooCommerce Widgets and Shortcodes

You can easily add handy functional bits to your shop using WooCommerce widgets.

If you go to *Appearance -> Widgets* from your Dashboard main menu, you'll see a bunch of cool WooCommerce widgets below the default WordPress widgets. You can place WooCommerce widgets wherever your theme displays a widgetized sidebar.

Here's just a selection of the widgets WooCommerce provides right out of the box:

- **Woo Adspace Widget** — use this widget to display ads in your online shop
- **Woo Flickr** — use this widget to display photos from your Flickr feed. Just enter your *Flickr ID* and the widget will do the rest
- **WooCommerce Cart** — this widget displays the contents of your customers' shopping cart
- **WooCommerce Price Filter** — this widget lets your customers filter products by price

- **WooCommerce Products** — this widget displays a list of your products
- **WooCommerce Product Categories** — this widget displays a list or drop-down box of product categories to help your customers get to what they're looking for quickly and easily.

To learn more, read the WooCommerce docs and experiment with all WooCommerce widgets in your own WordPress installation.

WordPress shortcodes are great for embedding content, creating layout structures, displaying recent posts, etc. without the hassle of having to learn some coding language or mess with themes or plugins files. WordPress has some useful built-in shortcodes, themes and plugins can extend WordPress by adding their own custom shortcodes.

A shortcode has a few possible formats:

- **[simple_shortcode]** — this is the simplest version of a shortcode. For instance, here's the WordPress shortcode to add the default gallery to a post or page: [gallery]
- **[shortcode_with_attributes   attribute1="value1" attribute2="value2"]** — this is a shortcode that specifies some attributes or arguments. For instance, you can use the same gallery shortcode above with some additional attributes to create an image gallery with no links, a two-column layout, and two photos that have an ID of 60 and 56 respectively: [gallery link="none" columns="2" ids="60,56"]
- **[shortcode_with_end_tag]some   content here[/shortcode_with_end_tag]** — this format is usually

for shortcodes which wrap content inside some HTML structure. For instance, a custom shortcode (not a default one that comes with WordPress) with an end tag could look something like this: [one_column]This paragraph will be displayed in one column on the page. [/one_column]. You wouldn't need to know the HTML and CSS required to build the column layout because the shortcode handles it for you.

WooCommerce has its own custom shortcodes that you can leverage in your own shop.

For instance, some of the pages WooCommerce creates automatically during the setup process are built using shortcodes. To show you this, go to *Pages -> All Pages* from the Dashboard main menu to open the *Pages* screen. From here, click the *Edit* link below the *Cart* page:

This will open the *Cart* page in the WordPress editor. As you can see, the simple [woocommerce_cart] shortcode is enough to generate the entire contents and structure of the shopping cart on your website.

Other WooCommerce shortcodes are:

[woocommerce_my_account] — to display your customer's *Account* page

[woocommerce_checkout] — to display the *Checkout* page

[woocommerce_thankyou] — to display the *Order Received* page

To dive into all the shortcodes WooCommerce makes available to you, head over to the WooCommerce docs.

WooCommerce Reports

WooCommerce offers some excellent reporting capabilities to keep you on top of everything that goes on with your online shop.

You access the *Reports* screen from *WooCommerce -> Reports* in the Dashboard main menu:

Build Your Own WordPress Website

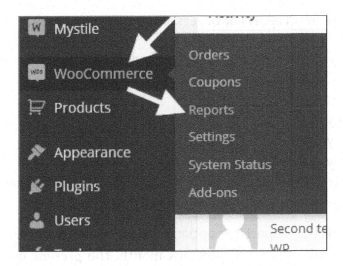

The *Reports* screen offers several options:

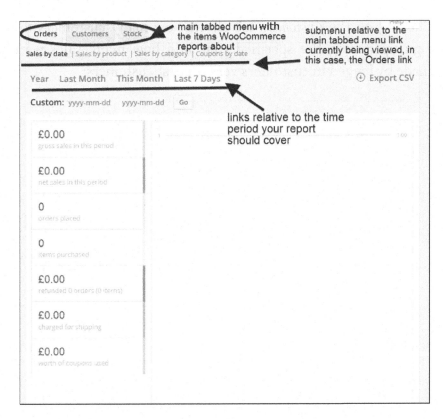

You can view reports of Orders, Customers and Stock.

When you click on the *Orders* tabbed menu link, you can view reports on your sales:

- By date
- By product
- By category
- And sales you've promoted using coupons organized by date

Each of the reporting options listed above, can be viewed relative to a year, the previous month, the present month, or the last seven days.

Clicking on the *Customers* tab shows how many customers did sign up during the specified time and how many sales were made by logged in customers versus guest customers:

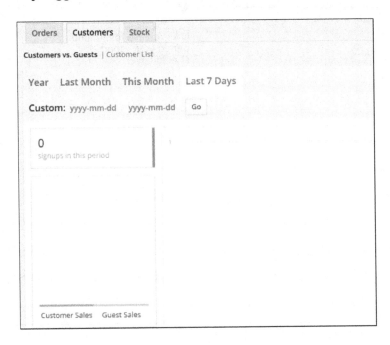

If you click on *Customer List*, you'll have a detailed overview of all your customers.

Finally, clicking on the *Stock* tabbed menu link reveals information about your stock in your selected period of time:

- Low in stock items
- Out of stock items
- Most stocked items

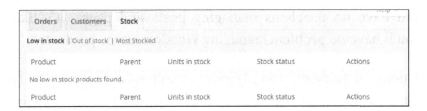

Going over each reporting feature WooCommerce makes available is beyond the scope of this chapter. To learn more, visit the WooCommerce Reports documentation page.

Conclusion

This chapter was designed to show you what's possible with WooCommerce and how easy it is to start using this awesome plugin to set up an online shop on your small business website.

You learned about:

- Benefits of using the WooCommerce plugin on your WordPress website
- How to install WooCommerce and go through the quick setup wizard

- The advantage of using a WooCommerce-compatible theme
- The basics of how to manage WooCommerce categories and products
- The basics of WooCommerce tools for managing your shop.

WooCommerce is seamlessly integrated with WordPress, therefore WooCommerce features are implemented using the familiar WordPress user interface elements. In other words, if you have no problems managing posts and pages, it's likely you'll have no problem managing WooCommerce products.

A detailed guide on using WooCommerce would take us too far. But fear not. If you get stuck, head over to the WooCommerce 101 Video Series for detailed instructions on each task involved in setting up your online shop.

The next chapter is all about keeping your WordPress website up-to-date, from themes and plugins to the WordPress platform itself.

Take a well-deserved break, come back and dig in!

CHAPTER 7:

Keeping Your Website Up-to-date

In this chapter you're going to learn how to:

- Update your WordPress installation
- Update your WordPress theme
- Update your WordPress plugins

Let's get started!

7.1 Why You Should Always Update Your Website

WordPress is in constant development: bugs are being fixed, security patches added, user experience keeps getting better and better, new features are being integrated all the time, etc.

Being open source, WordPress boasts an impressive number of developers and users from all over the world who are committed to making the platform more awesome every day by submitting bug reports, fixing stuff, and reviewing features.

What this means is that new versions of WordPress crop up at a super fast pace. Both themes and plugins are required to work with the latest version of the platform, which means that you'll also be seeing new versions of your favorite theme and plugins being rolled out at a fast rate.

It's therefore no surprise that having a WordPress website comes with the task of having to keep up with the crazed development pace of the platform and its extensions.

The first and most important move to keep your WordPress website secure is to be on top of themes, plugins and WordPress updates. The process is usually quick and painless, but it's a good idea to start becoming accustomed to it sooner rather than later.

Updates notifications

As soon as there's anything to update in your WordPress install, your dashboard will look something like this:

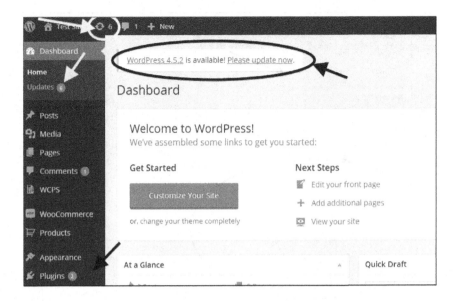

The dashboard notifies you of the overall updates you need to make as well as each specific component that needs updating.

You can also access the *Updates* page where you'll see different sections, each with one or more specific items to update.

You can manage all your updates from here:

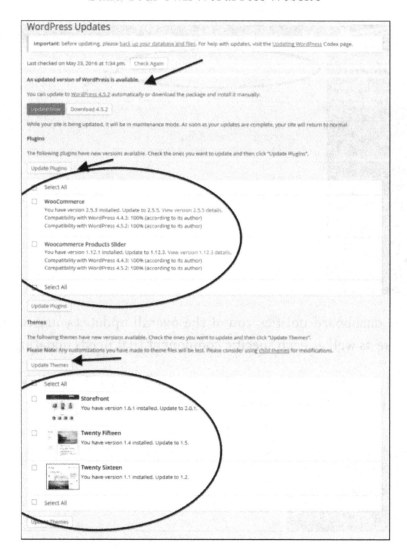

First, let's tackle updating WordPress itself!

7.2 How to Update Your WordPress Installation

Nowadays, you can quickly update to a new major versions of WordPress with a mouse click. You can also opt for the manual route, but I wouldn't recommend this if you're just starting out.

Here I'm going to show you how to perform a one-click install step by step. Manual updates are beyond the scope of this guide, but I'm going to point you to a number of useful online resources on how to go about it in the next chapter.

One more thing you need to know is that since WordPress version 3.7, minor updates like 3.7.1, 3.7.2, etc., execute automatically. No headaches, no hassle.

It's only for major feature releases that you need to do the updating yourself. Here's how.

Step #1: Backup your website

WordPress displays a notification at the top of the *Updates* page, which advises you to create a backup of your website before starting the update process.

WordPress Updates

Important: before updating, please back up your database and files. For help with updates, visit the Updating WordPress Codex page.

It's always wise to follow this tip because if something goes wrong during the update, your backup copy will save you from disaster.

To make your life easier, use any of the backup and restore plugins I discussed in Chapter 5. To read more about backing up WordPress, head over to this Codex article.

Step #2: Click on the Update Now Button

Click the big blue button that says "Update Now". That's all you need to do.

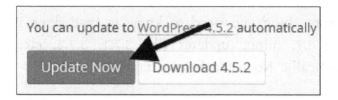

While updating, WordPress notifies you of each step in the process:

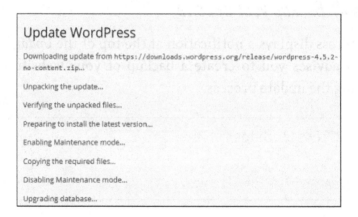

You can stay and watch, or you can simply grab a cup of coffee. By the time you're back, you should see something like this:

Welcome to WordPress 4.5.2

Thank you for updating! WordPress 4.5.2 streamlines your workflow, whether you're writing or building your site.

Version 4.5.2

At the time of writing, WordPress is at version 4.5.2. By the time you read this, it's likely the version number will have gone up quite a bit.

Congratulations, you've updated your WordPress website!

7.3 How to Update Your WordPress Theme

If you see a theme that doesn't get updated in a couple of years, this is a huge red flag. Theme updates concern improvements in the code base, security patches, bugs, compatibility issues with new versions of WordPress, new features, a fresher design, etc.

Getting your copy of the theme updated is also a matter of clicking a button. However, if you've customized your theme the wrong way, you could lose all your changes at one fell swoop.

The wrong way of customizing your WordPress theme

The worst possible thing you can do to your copy of a WordPress theme is to hack its files to make changes.

Although it might seem like the quickest method, it isn't, at least not in the long run.

The problem is that, when the time comes for you to update your copy of the theme, the one click update will wipe off all the changes you've made.

The alternative would be to track all the changes you've made, add them to the file in the updated version of the theme, then do a manual update. Not very practical, certainly not quick.

The right ways of customizing your WordPress theme

There are a few options of adding modifications to your theme without losing them on the next theme update.

The best way is using the **WordPress Customizer** (*Appearance -> Customize* from the main dashboard menu), which I showed in Chapter 4. This is also the easiest way of personalizing a theme.

However, not all themes offer great customization options via the Customizer. Or, the kind of modifications you'd like to add don't have any corresponding settings in the Customizer for the particular theme you're using.

If your changes only involve CSS styles like colors, fonts, backgrounds, etc., you're in luck. Adding style rules using a **custom CSS editor** is the next best option when the Customizer isn't enough for your needs. Some themes already come bundled with a custom CSS editor. If your theme is not one of them, there are plugins on the WordPress.org plugins repository that let you add a custom CSS editor in no time. Here are just a couple for your reference:

- Sublime Custom CSS Editor
- Custom CSS — Whole Site and Per Post

You can even use a plugin to add both more Customizer options and a custom CSS editor. Here's a great one: Customify — A Theme Customizer Booster.

Of course, you need to know at least a bit of CSS, the language that lets you control the appearance of your theme, to be able to carry out your modifications. But there are plenty of resources out there to get you started, some of which I'm going to give you in the next chapter.

The last option is to create a WordPress child theme. Child themes are themes based off of your chosen theme. As soon as they're created, they look exactly the same as your theme, which in this case is called **parent theme.** This is so because the child inherits everything from its parent. Child themes only need a *functions.php* file and a *style.css* file to work. To change the look and feel of your theme, add the necessary CSS code to *style.css* in your child theme. If you need to change the structure of a template file like the homepage or the comments list, etc., you need to copy over the relevant template file from the parent theme into the child theme and make your modifications in the child theme. To change any functionality, add your PHP code to *functions.php* in your child theme. Any file or function you modify in the child will override the parent's files. When it's time to update, you'll be updating only the parent theme, while your child theme will inherit the updates from the parent but keep your modifications safe. How to customize your website using a child theme is a bit more advanced than the options outlined above and is beyond the scope of this guide. The good news is that you'll find tons of references online on how to create and use child themes. I'm going to leave some relevant links in the following chapter.

One-click theme update

You can update your theme from the *Updates* page that you saw in the previous section, or from the *Themes* panel. Here's what the *Themes* panel looks like when a new version of your themes is available.

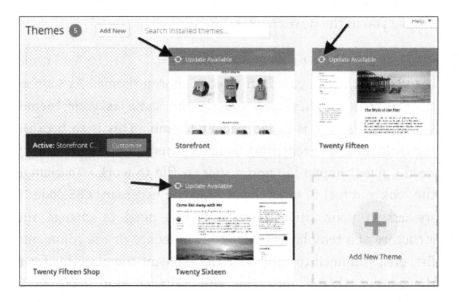

Just go ahead and click on the *Update Available* notice on the theme. If your theme is hosted on WordPress.org, the *Theme Details* panel opens up. Click the *update now* link and let WordPress do the hard work for you.

If everything goes according to plan, your screen should look something like this:

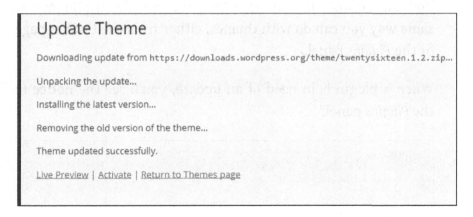

If you go back to the *Themes* panel, the update notice should have disappeared from the screen.

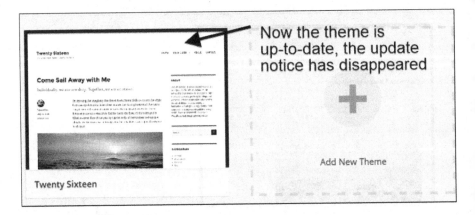

Now the theme is up-to-date, the update notice has disappeared

Add New Theme

Twenty Sixteen

If you bought your theme from a marketplace, just follow the instructions the vendor must have provided you with.

7.4 How to Update Your WordPress Plugins

You can do one-click updates for your WordPress plugins the same way you can do with themes, either from the *Updates* page or the *Plugins* panel.

When a plugin is in need of an update, you'll see the notice in the *Plugins* panel:

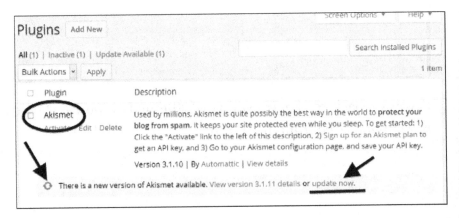

Click on the *update now* link and wait for the success message:

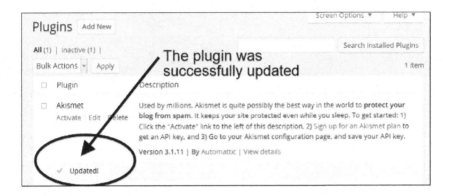

That's all there is to it!

If anything goes wrong during a theme or plugin update you can try again with the one-click method. If for some reason the update keeps failing, the alternative is a manual update, which involves downloading the theme or plugin files into your website's server using FTP. This is a more advanced approach which is not suited to someone who's not familiar with servers, FTP or WordPress. In this case, I advise you ask your hosting provider for help or hire a professional.

Conclusion

At the end of this chapter you've learned:

- How to update to the latest version of WordPress
- How to update your theme to its latest version
- How to update your plugins to their latest version.

The final chapter will be packed with links to great online resources where you can learn more about WordPress, find useful plugins, and get help.

CHAPTER 8:

Where to Learn More – Online Resources

In this chapter you'll find links to awesome online resources designed to help you learn more about WordPress, WooCommerce, themes and plugins. Building your website has never been more fun.

Obviously this book was written by a team of experts at Thewordpressgenie.com. So you should head over and take a look at the ever expanding list of articles, how to guides and books for businesses!

Enjoy!

8.1 WordPress Tutorials

The links below lead to tons of tutorials on installing, using and updating WordPress, on themes and child themes, plugins, and where to get more help.

The WordPress Codex

The WordPress Codex is the master manual on everything relating to WordPress. If in doubt about anything, just type your question together with the word 'codex' into your favourite search engine, and 99% of the times you'll find your answer.

Here's a list of references to the most common WordPress-related topics.

- Download WordPress
- Installing WordPress
- Getting Started with WordPress
- WordPress Lessons
- Creating and Using Posts
- Creating and Using Pages
- Using Themes
- Using Plugins
- Using Permalinks
- Theme Development
- Child Themes
- Blog Design and Layout

Other sources of general WordPress tutorials

The Codex is the official WordPress manual, therefore I recommend you check it out before trusting any other source. However, it's not terribly user-friendly, especially for beginners. If you're looking for something that looks a bit less intimidating, here's a list of places worth visiting.

- WordPress 101 Videos by WordPress Beginner
- WordPress Tutorials on WordPress Beginner
- WordPress Tutorial by SiteGround
- WordPress 101 by iThemes
- A Guide to WordPress for Beginners by Udemy
- WordPress Tutorial for Beginners - Video by WebsiteWizard.tv

Forums for extra-WordPress help

- WordPress.org Support Forums
- WordPress Stack Exchange
- WordPress IRC Live Help
- CSS-Tricks Forums
- WordPress.com Support Forums

WordPress themes

- How to Install a WordPress Theme by WordPress Beginner
- How to Install WordPress Themes by SiteGround
- Installing and Activating Your Premium WordPress Theme by GoDaddy

WordPress Child Theme

- Child Theme Basics by The Theme Foundry

- How To Create A Child Theme, And Why You Should Be Using One by Elegant Themes
- What is a WordPress Child Theme? Pros, Cons, and More by WordPress Beginner

WordPress Plugins

- How to Install a WordPress Plugin - Step by Step for Beginners by WordPress Beginner
- How to Use WordPress Plugins by Website Magazine
- 7 Things You Should Know About Using WordPress Plugins by WPExplorer
- Best WordPress Plugins 2016 by WordPress Beginner

8.2 WooCommerce Tutorials

WooCommerce is the most popular ecommerce plugin for WordPress. Chapter 6 was all about setting up a small shop on your WordPress website. For more WooCommerce help and demos, follow the links below.

- WooCommerce Documentation by WooThemes
- WooCommerce 101 Video Tutorials - Build your store from start to sale! By WooThemes
- Storefront: How To Make An Ecommerce WordPress Website - On A Budget Video by Katrinah
- How to Setup WordPress WooCommerce - Complete Tutorial by WPDean

8.3 Where You Can Get WordPress Themes and Plugins

There are tons of places offering both free and paid themes and plugins for WordPress. Here's a list of well-established marketplaces with a great selection of themes and plugins to choose from and safely use on your WordPress website.

- WordPress.org Themes (Free Themes)
- WordPress.org Plugins (Free Plugins)
- ThemeForest (Paid Themes Marketplace)
- CodeCanyon (Paid Plugins Marketplace)
- Mojo Themes (Paid Themes Marketplace)
- Mojo Code (Paid Plugins Marketplace)
- Elegant Themes (Paid Themes and Plugins Marketplace)
- iThemes (Paid Themes and Plugins, Training, and More)
- Theme Hybrid (A WordPress Themes and Plugins Club)
- WPEden (Free and Paid WordPress Themes and Plugins)
- Codester (Paid Themes and Plugins)

8.4 WordPress Hosting

Most hosting providers offer WordPress hosting and one-click WordPress install. Here's a few of the major ones.

- HostGator
- DreamHost
- GoDaddy
- SiteGround
- BlueHost
- MediaTemple

Conclusion

Congratulations, you've come to the end of your journey to building a small business website with WordPress.

If you've followed along, you should have your own WordPress website up and running. If not, what are you waiting for?

Keep in mind that building your website is just the first step. To make that website work for your business, you'll need to

- Keep it up-to-date, bugs-free and secure
- Add great copy
- Learn the secrets of blogging
- Promote your website on influential blogs and social media
- Track users' actions and making adjustments to improve results

Need help and want to learn more?

Here's how you can get in touch with us:

info@thewordpressgenie.com

Visit thewordpressgenie.com

If you've found my guide useful, let's make the web even more awesome and share its title with your friends :)

Built your website but want to learn more on SEO? Please check out our SEO: For small businesses guide, we feel it compliments this book beautifully. Check it out at our website thewordpressgenie.com or on Amazon.

The link on our website is:
http://thewordpressgenie.com/books-and-guides/

Thank you for reading and keep growing your business with WordPress!

CPSIA information can be obtained
at www.ICGtesting.com
Printed in the USA
LVOW05s1746220817

545954LV00013B/965/P